WORKS OF HEART

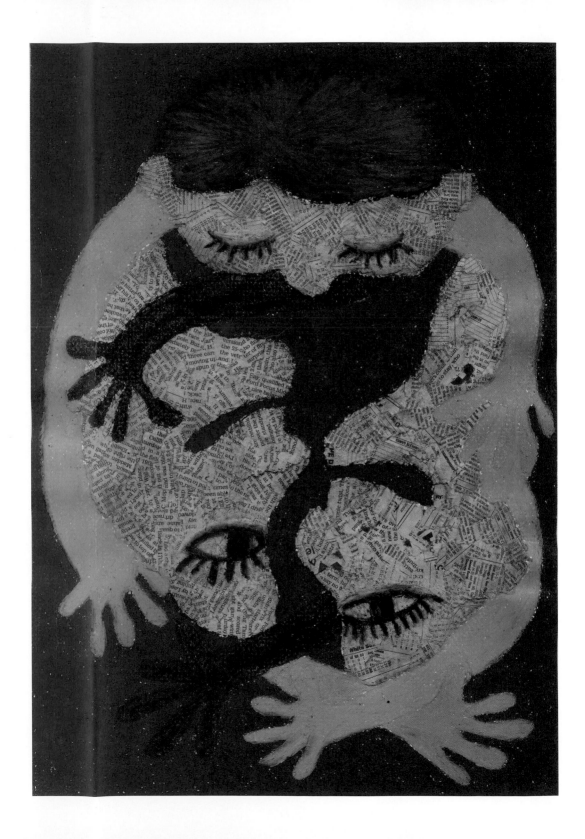

WORKS OF HEART

Building Village Through the Arts

LYNNE ELIZABETH
SUZANNE YOUNG
EDITORS

newvillagePRESS

Oakland, California

Works of Heart: Building Village Through the Arts

Published by
New Village Press
P.O. Box 3049
Oakland, CA 94609
Orders: (510) 420-1361
press@newvillage.net
www.newvillagepress.net

New Village Press books are published under the auspices of
Architects/Designers/Planners for Social Responsibility.
www.adpsr.org

Printed and bound in China.
First printing, September 2006.

Library of Congress Cataloging-in-Publication Data

Works of heart : building village through the arts / editors, Lynne Elizabeth
and Suzanne Young ; introduction, Thomas Borrup.
       p. cm.
  Includes index.
  ISBN-13: 978-0-9766054-0-9 (hardcover : alk. paper)
  ISBN-10: 0-9766054-0-6 (hardcover : alk. paper)
  1. Community development--Case studies. 2. Community arts projects--
Case studies. I. Elizabeth, Lynne. II. Young, Suzanne.
  HN49.C6W68 2006
  700.97--dc22
                                        2006009582

Front cover photo: Lily Yeh, Village of Arts and Humanities, Philadelphia.
Back cover photo: Village of Arts and Humanities, Philadelphia

Dedicated to Jane Jacobs (1916–2006)

*"You have to love your city and love
the area you're trying to improve,
genuinely love it . . ."*

Contents

Acknowledgements

Works of Heart and New Village Press have been blessed with the generous help of many. Linda Frye Burnham, community arts guru and co-director of the stupendous online hub—the Community Arts Network—connected us to the movers and shakers in the field. Karen Kearney, right arm with the Press, has brought patience and kindness beyond the call. Graphic artist Robin Terra designed the first chapter that set the book's lively visual tone. Developer Merritt Sher graciously provided free office space while the journal found new wings as the Press. Allan McAllister, Suzanne Young's husband donated many late nights creating our financial spreadsheets. Chris Plant, principal of New Society Publishers supplied ready advice of a seasoned publisher, and Consortium, our brilliant distributor, is still teaching us the ropes.

Other helpers include Tia Stoller and staff who designed the beautiful logo and website for New Village Press, "thinking partner" Mary Jane Ryan, proofreader Nancy Bauer, and Bernard Marszalek and Terry O'Keefe for ongoing marketing ideas and moral support.

Works of Heart and the Press have been generously gifted with grants. Seed funders include the National Endowment for the Arts, the Graham Foundation for Advanced Studies in the Arts, the Educational Foundation of America, and the Nathan Cummings Foundation. Individuals have helped, too—Jonathan Frieman, Joanni Blank and Michael Pyatok. Thank you!

We are most especially grateful to the contributing authors and the organizations and artists whose work is here displayed. May this book honor their creativity as their creativity honors the communities they serve.

Preface

The word love is not commonly used among planners and community development specialists who cautiously measure the "social capital" of "civil society," so we laud the late Jane Jacobs, to whom this book is dedicated, for speaking up about that gutsy emotion that truly makes the world go 'round. Communities that "get it" express a central vibrancy so irresistible, their good work is self-perpetuating. Such zeal, such neighborhood caring, is the stuff this book is made of.

Indeed, community is not really built from budgets and plans, nor is it a product of monthly meetings, however much these contribute. It is born, rather, out of a deep and natural passion to make the world a better place for those we cherish—a healthier, more congenial place, where we can grow and express who we really are or who we'd like to be. *Works of Heart* celebrates the genius of citizens who have risked seeming foolish and discovered the joy of playing together to create and recreate community in artistic ways—through puppets, parades, murals, sculpture, drumming, banners, acrobatics, architectural renovation, opera, drama, painting and poetry.

Works of Heart was initially conceived as a themed issue of *New Village Journal* about strengthening communities through the arts. The material we began assembling was so gorgeous, however, we could only imagine publishing it in color, which led us to imagine publishing it as a book. Seeing that these stories, magnificent as they are, were mere morsels in a banquet of untold stories led to the greater idea of turning the journal into a full-fledged book-publishing concern that could focus on grassroots community building.

And so, this book comes to you now through New Village Press in the happy company of other wonderful books, all born of love.

SOAP FACTORY INTERIOR
BEFORE RENOVATION. (SEE
SAVING THE SOAP, PP. 30-42.)
PHOTO BY HEATHER BEAL.

Introduction

Creating Community with What's Underfoot

Tom Borrup

We tend to underestimate what is close at hand—the ground under our feet, broken glass, a flurry of conversation at the market, an empty factory. Who pays attention to ordinary or discarded items? Artists do. They notice the sights, sounds and experiences of everyday life and use them as source materials. They find value in what others overlook.

It's a deeply human capacity to create from what is at hand or underfoot. Yet for most of us, the creative impulse lies buried beneath the surface. We are content to be the recipients of creativity and culture without delving into the mud to make things ourselves. The artists in this book all share a common quality: They bring together generosity of the heart with the ability to dig deep to find the vision, the wherewithal and the raw materials to improve life in the communities and world in which they live.

Artists invent new ways to approach sickness, to repair the distressed planet and to bridge differences. They connect us with our common humanity and our individual histories and truths. Through the arts we can more deeply understand where we live. And when artists and community work together wonderful things happen.

Recognizing this, poet and co-founder of California's River of Words, Robert Hass, states in the pages that follow, "We need both things—a living knowledge of the land and a live imagination of it and our place in it."

Hass, and others whose stories are told here, join artists around the world who collaborate and do remarkable work to advance such goals as social and environmental justice, health, human rights and cross-cultural bridge building. They find ingenious ways to draw on the essence of place, of people and of cultural heritage. Bringing this essence together with creative imagination, these community-based artists catalyze people, visions and energies. They weave a synergistic social fabric while tackling complex local and global issues.

This work goes by many names: cultural activism, arts-based community building or community cultural development. I also use "asset-based community organizing" and "creative community building." Whatever it's called, it taps into the deep well of assets and strengths people and communities have and builds on them.

The cultures, traditions, artistic pursuits and the stories of where people come from and what they believe in are among the assets artists bring to the table of social change work. They join with others who bring recycled materials, plants, crafts, science, organizing skills and other resources. Together they create, build, re-build and celebrate. In the stories that follow—and there are so many others like them—artists are collaborating to utilize the assets at hand.

Youth in Oregon literally make mud and, in a remarkable process rooted in ancient African traditions, create beauty in their bleak built environment. Cuts in school budgets prompt artist Kiko Denzer to draw on raw material that's beneath his feet—the most common building material on the planet—to engage kids in designing and creating colorful mud murals that transform a dull school building into something vibrant.

At Philadelphia's Village of Arts & Humanities, a process of aesthetic transformation brightens the outlook of residents who, in turn, rebuild both the physical structures and the social fabric of their community. Teenagers in this 100-square-block section of North Philadelphia symbolically and in reality become what founder Lily Yeh calls, "guardians of the earth" and "torchbearers of the future."

Environmentally-conscious artists looking for materials with which to convert an old industrial building into an alternative art center in Minneapolis helped to dismantle an about-to-be-demolished shopping mall. They called upon neighbors, local businesses, professional groups and their own ingenuity. In so doing they pulled off a remarkable environmental reuse demonstration and community-building project. "No one who has worked on this project will ever view buildings the same way again," former group leader Heather Beal writes.

Community-based arts practitioners respond creatively to their environment, recognizing and raising up important and otherwise unheard or unseen stories, resources and talents. They mobilize assets and advance social-justice and social-change efforts at the same time. Practitioners and funders in community development and social-change work are widely adopting this strategy, and its terms have become part of the lexicon.

While people working in the arts seem less familiar with these terms, they are often the most adept practitioners. They take raw materials and imaginatively enhance them or adapt them to other uses. Beginning with any manner of mate-

HAND PAINTED MEMORIAL POLES AT THE VILLAGE OF ARTS AND HUMANITIES, NORTH PHILADELPHIA.

rials, artists create beauty, profound meaning and worth well beyond the value of the ingredients. They transform words, sounds, images, movements, objects, even lives and entire city blocks.

In creating the Garden of Hope, artist and cancer patient Ann Chamberlain started with her imagination. She looked at a dreary hospital courtyard and asked, "Why isn't this a garden?" She and her doctor began to organize a small effort and, as people saw change and the potential, interest grew. Eventually the stark, unused courtyard was transformed into a remarkable place of beauty, restoration and learning about herbal and other therapies. Those involved gained new relationships, tools and reasons to persevere.

Artists, teachers and students in California's River of Words, blend poetry, art, nature study, watershed awareness, community service, history and critical thinking. Through a new curriculum they grow both poets and engaged citizens. Alicia Hokanson says she teaches poetry "because I want poets running my neighborhood council, my city, my country... I want a richer world for all of us—where the truths of the eye and the heart are valued more than those of the pocketbook."

Members of Maine's Beehive Design Collective were intrigued with the aesthetic qualities of an old boarded-up farmers meeting hall. They began to restore it with the vision of serving as an all-ages community arts and education center to "cross-pollinate the grassroots." Only after beginning the process, did they discover the rich political and social history of the Grange movement, embodied by the historic building. And, they found they had values in common with it. Through their process they built connections across generations, social movements and neighbors.

Fundamentally, asset-based work is about fostering the capacity to see, cultivate and use power a community didn't know it had. It's about seeing the world and approaching the work from a position of strength rather than weakness, and it's about taking initiative.

Most of today's nonprofit and civic leaders have been trained to see problems and shortcomings as the starting point for change-making, fundraising and organizational development. The artists and art projects in this book are among the many who challenge these deficit-based models. They see themselves existing in a world where everyone is rich—at least in culture, traditions and talents.

Theater artist Annie Rachele Lanzillotto finds that the old Bronx Marketplace that meant so much to her ailing mother was really a catalyst for memories, old stories and songs. She learned to "embrace the cacophony as an expression of pluralism." With help from grants and friends, she transformed the Market into a theatrical space and event. Vendors and customers become the cast and transactions become the drama. She built on its rhythms and aesthetics, connecting people and cultures in astonishing ways. In the end she describes herself as an "Interaction Practitioner."

Clara Wainwright, Boston-based public celebration artist, quiltmaker and founder of the Faith Quilts Project, used a different technique towards a similar end. She found both difference and commonality right in her own neighborhood and that the process of making quilts with people from different traditions could connect them through reflection, verbal exchange and the creation of something visually expressive.

"It's every kind of people, they come from everywhere, and they come to take a chance on magic," writer Kate Madden Yee says of people turning out for Vancouver's summer multicultural festival of light. Community artists of the Public Dreams Society create celebrations to spark connections among neighbors, to entice them to play together through performances, festivals and rituals, rooted in the many cultures of this cosmopolitan city.

Like art itself, asset-based practices are a discipline. And they are where cultural practice intersects with progressive community organizing and development. Cultural intermediaries partnered with organizers and advocates sharing similar values can bring new levels of effectiveness to social-justice and social change endeavors. Seeing assets, rather than deficits in each other and in the places we inhabit, provides highly productive ground on which to build. It engenders a more energetic spirit with which to approach problems.

Driven by creative impulses, artists never stop learning and exploring new ideas and ways of doing things. In applying themselves to social change work, the artists of the Beehive Design Collective recognized there's never a finish line for the work they do. Visions of what might be and the raw materials with which to realize them are always in abundance among creative community builders like these in the following pages.
♥

CREATING PLACE

Song of the Wounded Earth

To remember, to mourn, to heal, to celebrate

S U Z A N N E   Y O U N G

STRONG COLORS AND
BOLD GEOMETRY, INFUSED
WITH A JOYOUS SENSE OF
EXPRESSION, CARRIED THE
KUJENGA PAMOJA FESTIVAL'S
MESSAGE TO HONOR THE
LAND, THE AIR, THE OCEAN
AND ALL LIVING CREATURES.
THE FESTIVAL WAS THE
CULMINATION OF A YEAR'S
WORTH OF ART-BASED PROJ-
ECTS INVOLVING HUNDREDS
OF CHILDREN, TEENS
AND ADULTS.

The glittering mosaics and visual beauty of the Village of Arts and Humanities would be vibrant in any context. But after passing through block after city block of grime-blackened houses in North Philadelphia, the defeated soil of rubble-strewn lots gives way to an enclave. Here the sense of energy and order is startling in its incongruity. Color is everywhere. The heart of the Village, a ten-square-block area deep within North Philadelphia, radiates sparks of energy the way a diamond catches the light. Abandoned lots are reclaimed into gardens; low, undulating walls surround tiled courtyards. Fledgling trees grow in precise rows in a community nursery. Mosaics and wall murals in primary colors announce that a vital spirit is at work.

Founder Lily Yeh, an artist who answered an invitation to create a garden in an abandoned lot here in 1986 and then somehow never left, has nurtured that first garden into an entire Village. In the Village today, more than 250 abandoned lots and structures have become 24 parks, gardens and green spaces. There are at least a half dozen rehabbed houses and six brand new ones, not to mention sustainable enterprises, such as the nursery with up to 15,000 seedlings and a crafts studio. Since its inception, the Village has grown to include a permanent staff, an annual budget of $1.3 million, and hundreds of volunteers. From its 10-block heart, it serves a 260-block area. But its influence extends even further, through the groups of college students who learn community building firsthand by tackling volunteer projects at the Village and through the community development professionals around the world who come to watch and understand.

Under the inspired direction of Yeh, the staff, student volunteers and a growing core of leading artists help children and teens learn skills, make art and express themselves. In the process, they are rebuilding a shattered community, one mosaic chip at a time.

"In places like North Philadelphia, art is even more powerful," Yeh says. "Here, it is the cement that holds the community together."

In 2002, a year's worth of economic development, skill building and art projects came together in the Village's annual fall Kujenga Pamoja festival. Well before the events of September 11, 2001, Village staff had adopted the theme "Song of the Wounded Earth" for the next year's festival, to acknowledge the vulnerability of the earth, the air and the water. By the time the festival took place in late September 2002, the theme had acquired even deeper resonance.

Although the annual festival always has a spontaneous, even chaotic feel, it is carefully choreographed. The staff develops a detailed plan of event sequences throughout the multi-block festival area, beginning with the 10 a.m. technical and physical set-ups, to the 4 p.m. launch, through its conclusion at around 9 p.m.

VILLAGE FOUNDER LILY YEH FINDS MUCH TO CELEBRATE IN A ONCE-DERELICT NEIGHBORHOOD. THE TRANSFORMING POWER OF ART IS IN EVIDENCE EVERYWHERE IN THE TEN-SQUARE-BLOCK VILLAGE HEART.

KUJENGA PAMOJA During Lily Yeh's first visit to Nairobi, the Village motto "Together We Build" captured the hearts of the people in one of Nairobi's poorest neighborhoods. On her return, she dubbed the Village's annual festival "Kujenga Pamoja," which is the motto's Swahili translation.

Kujenga Pamoja 2002 began with the arrival of a drill team from another North Philadelphia neighborhood, who had marched sixteen blocks in formation to the festival to announce to the Village that it was time to begin.

"Their energy was just heart boiling," Yeh said. "They really started us off."

Hundreds of villagers mingled with hundreds of visitors "to remember, to mourn, to heal, to celebrate." Three Village parks, all former lots reclaimed from neglect, carried the festival theme's three components: earth, air and ocean. Children and parents decorated the parks with crepe paper streamers, fashioned musical instruments out of bean pods, old milk cartons and pots and pans to hang from the trees, made headdresses, painted their faces, and added last-minute touches to the animal costumes.

With the final preparations now finished, the crowd assembled in the Village heart for a "blessing procession." Among those in the throng were parents, children, community officials including the mayor of Philadelphia and the district's state senator, and visitors from as far away as Colorado and Taiwan. The assembly promenaded through the Village, past a forest of memorial poles, stopping at a dozen or so houses to bestow blessings and good will.

"May the Great Spirit bless this household," someone called, and the crowd chanted it back in unison. "And bless these children. And bless this family. And may the Great Spirit bless this village." A child stepped forward to offer a bright

basket filled with flowers and vegetables to the residents gathered at the front door. Handfuls of glitter and confetti sprayed the air; the crowd cheered and then moved on to the next house. The mayor gamely wore a Village-made flowered headdress and led the blessings for several houses himself.

The entourage made its way to the three parks. The low walls, trees and fountains were now decorated with crepe paper streamers, which the wind set to fluttering, while digital music created by Village teens played in the background. Their blessings honored the work of the construction crews, community volunteers, Village artisans and children who had worked together to create these islands of beauty and order.

In front of a debris-filled lot, the procession stopped in the waning afternoon. Yeh said, "Here we need a really, really big blessing for this land, so we can get the funding to

rudy bruner award

THE VILLAGE OF ARTS AND HUMANITIES was Gold Medal winner of the 2001 Rudy Bruner Award for Urban Excellence. The biennial Rudy Bruner Award honors places developed with such vision and imagination that they transform urban problems into creative solutions. Award winners are innovative and guided by creative visions of what is possible, often in defiance of existing norms. Many reflect complex collaborations among people who may not have come together before. Awardees, like the Village of Arts and Humanities, often have succeeded, under the most adverse conditions imaginable, in creating places that become the cornerstones of their communities.

The Rudy Bruner Award for Urban Excellence was established in 1986 by Simeon Bruner and named in honor of his late father. Simeon Bruner, himself, has been a leader in urban arhitecture, pioneering adaptive reuse of historic 19th and early 20th century buildings. His urban renovation projects include the Massachusetts Museum of Contemporary Art (MASS MoCA) in North Adams.

Each Rudy Bruner Award cycle documents awardees in a set of detailed case studies that include project history, financing, design, impact and other measures of success. Rudy Bruner Award books may be ordered through the Bruner Foundation at www.brunerfoundation.org

restore it." The crowd mustered up even more energy for that blessing.

It was dusk when the procession ended back in the heart of the Village, where participants did what people do at every festival the world over: they ate. After the substantial meal, everyone converged at Ile Ife Park, the Village's first park, where the children donned costumes. Accompanied by street marshals, the drill team led the now-large crowd across Germantown Avenue, a major thoroughfare, to a large abandoned lot. "An enchanted land," Yeh called it, which had been transformed into a ceremonial ground lit with lanterns. Here, the three-story brick wall of a bordering abandoned building became a 60-foot wide screen for a video show of some of nature's most dramatic scenes, interwoven with footage of the Village's children. Projected in large-scale were crashing waves caught in mid-spray, a field of brilliant wildflowers amid lush grass, mountain peaks and more.

"You know where the word breathtaking comes from when you hear the audience gasp at the images," Yeh said. "The beauty of these huge images literally takes their breath away. They have never seen such beauty in their neighborhood. And yet, here it is, right in front of them."

A low pulse of African drums introduced the Ivory Coast's leading dancer and choreographer, who launched a youth theater piece around the festival's theme of the relationship between people and the earth at this moment in human history. The children, costumed as animals, fish and birds, chanted their theme songs. Children from the poetry workshops recited their poems, against a background of music created by Village youth and arranged by a resident composer. Accompanied by drums, the teens, garbed in white robes with red sashes, moved from the back of the field to the stage down front for the ceremony that mourned the wounded earth.

MEMORIAL POLES (RIGHT) COMBINE POETRY WITH VIBRANT GEOMETRICS. ARCHITECTURE STUDENTS FROM THE UNIVERSITY OF PENNSYLVANIA HELPED THE VILLAGE "PLANT" A FOREST OF THE FOUR- TO EIGHT-FOOT POLES.

Here, candles held high against the dark, Village teenagers were initiated as the new guardians of the earth. Torchbearers of the future, they swore an oath to protect the land and to respect the creatures and the people in it.

"Symbolically, we introduce the teens into the program with the support of the witnesses. We are the witnesses," Yeh said. "We are weaving this so tight that they cannot fall through."

The festival culminated with nearly everyone dancing on stage in happy abandon.

As it turned out, "Song of the Wounded Earth" was the most successful Kujenga Pamoja festival ever. To figure out why, Yeh and her staff evaluated every aspect of the festival. The difference between success and disappointment certainly wasn't the amount of work that went into it, year after year. Ultimately, they concluded that incorporating the work done by various groups during the year into the festival made it a culmination and celebration of the year by many, rather than a special event done by a few. Even those who could not attend were represented by their work on costumes, poetry or music, much of it done in the Village's summer workshops.

"This is an all-inclusive creative process that anyone can interpret and follow their own passion in interpretation. It is multi-layered. Everyone's creative energy is included and honored. And it's a lot of fun and togetherness. It culminates in such imagination and beauty of art," Yeh said.

Yeh says that "community building is not just about housing, although we are doing that. It's not just about gardens, but that's an important backbone here. It's not just about education. It's about all of that but…" she stops and then picks up again in a quiet voice. "We must remember our heart and our soul and our emotion. You create structure for people to express themselves and you do it at a professional level."

Indeed, the artists that have attached themselves to the Village are a notable group that includes dance, theater, film and music professionals, all acclaimed in their fields. "People think community-based art is not good. But we make it the best. At this professional level," Yeh says, "through art we transform the grittiness of everyday life into energy, beauty, joy, strength, to help us face the future."

Slowly, people are returning to the neighborhood because it is safer. An alley where drug dealers once dominated is now dubbed Angel Alley, for the wall-high Ethiopian angels in brilliant mosaics, some with fierce swords, who stand guard over the community. As abandoned houses are rehabbed by the Village or removed and turned into gardens, the drug trade recedes and with it, the crime. The Village's tree nursery in a once-abandoned field across the street from a high-rise low-income housing project has no fences, yet.

"I don't say that this is not without a struggle," Yeh says. "Building a sustainable program in the inner city is like building a castle on quicksand. It's very hard, but we keep at it, we keep at it. Many times we fall flat on our faces, but when we do it right, there's nothing like it. Nothing like it." ♥

The Village of Arts and Humanities celebrated its 20th anniversary in June 2006 with a gala Kujenga Pamoja / Juntos Construimos / Together We Build Festival.

Kumani Gant, Executive Director
Village of Arts and Humanities
2544 Germantown Avenue
Philadelphia, PA 19133
www.villagearts.org

barefoot artists

IN 2003, LILY YEH FORMED Barefoot Artists, Inc., a non-
profit arts organization that uses the power of art to
transform impoverished communities. Based on her 18
years of work in the Village of Arts and Humanities in
North Philadelphia, she has taken the concepts and models
proven there, and, through Barefoot Artists, applied them
in projects in Kenya, Ghana, Ecuador, China and Rwanda,
among others.

As the name implies, Barefoot Artists is a volunteer organization without the encumbrance of permanent staff
and overhead, for which Yeh is the unpaid founder and
lead artist. She contracts for services as needed, and raises
funds for specific projects that pair volunteer expertise
with local people to advance health, education and economic development.

"Warrior Angel: The Work of Lily Yeh" by Bill Moskin and
Jill Jackson, a paper on her methodology of using art to
transform and build community, can be found at www.
barefootartists.org

Barefoot Artists
P.O. Box 2348
Philadelphia, PA 19103

Saving the Soap

HEATHER BEAL

Was it imagination and persistence, or just sheer naiveté? To this day, I'm still not sure what led the board of our budding arts group to believe we could dismantle the usable materials from an $74 million shopping center to transform an abandoned riverfront factory into a worthy arts space.

A gallery for emerging artists, No Name Exhibitions fills a niche in the Minneapolis arts community by presenting exceptional, often provocative, art in a wide range of media and forms. Our sprawling nineteenth-century building in Marcy Holmes, the city's oldest neighborhood, once housed the National Purity Soap Company, one of many such operations in this gritty industrial area. Today, this building we named The Soap Factory is home to No Name's galleries and administrative offices, which occupy a now-prime location in a riverfront area rapidly changing from industrial to mixed-use. When we began the factory's gradual transformation—an expensive undertaking, especially for our organization which had little cash—the neighborhood had barely begun to change. Yet, we forged ahead with the support of more than one hundred volunteers, a dozen local companies, the Minnesota Office of Environmental Assistance (OEA) and various private and public foundations. In hindsight, our timing was ideal.

Shortly after Pillsbury/Grand Met donated the factory to us in 1995, we realized the building would require code-mandated improvements to become the multi-use arts center we envisioned. Exterior priorities included a new roof, replacing hundreds of broken windowpanes and repairing the masonry. On the inside, the building needed everything from fire sprinkler heads, exit signs and fire doors to bathroom partitions, railings, ceramic tile and sinks.

Because No Name was a young arts organization (created in 1988) and we supported emerging rather than established artists, we had yet to develop the individual donor base and the revenue streams of major visual arts venues. It was clear we'd have to find creative sources for donated materials and equipment. Out of this need, we engineered the fortuitous intersection between the demise of a once-glamorous shopping mall and the rebirth of our abandoned factory.

ALTHOUGH THE MARBLE
CLADDING ON THE
CONSERVATORY'S GRAND
ATRIA STAIRWAYS WAS
TOO THIN AND TOO FIRMLY
ADHERED TO BE SALVAGE-
ABLE, CREWS WERE ABLE
TO SUCCESSFULLY REMOVE
MARBLE FROM THE FLOOR
SURFACE BELOW.

In the heart of downtown Minneapolis, a shopping center called The Conservatory had fallen on hard times. Opened in 1987 to great fanfare with its marble, granite, slate, brass and custom cast iron finishes, this center was touted as Minneapolis' version of Chicago's Water Tower Place. While the Conservatory made possible the Twin Cities' debut of national specialty retailers, it never achieved the occupancy levels required to survive. Six years after it opened, it was sold for a fraction of its original value. During the next three years, the new owner proposed various ideas for the center's reuse but none proved feasible. As news broke that a national developer, Ryan Companies US, was planning to purchase the Conservatory and demolish it to make way for a new office tower, No Name's board of directors had just begun to realize the magnitude of the improvements our former factory building would require.

My curiosity propelled me to take a walk through the Conservatory and I began making a list of items that could live a long and useful life at the Soap Factory. When I ran the idea of deconstructing pieces of the Conservatory by friends and professional colleagues, their reactions ranged from "bold and fascinating" to "out there" and "just plain crazy." Yet it was this bold and crazy project No Name spent the next several years orchestrating and completing. A remarkable series of circumstances made deconstruction and reuse a viable option for us.

When I presented the formal deconstruction and reuse plan to No Name's board, everyone agreed I should contact Ryan Companies to ask if our volunteers could salvage what we needed. Fortunately for us, Ryan is headquartered in Minneapolis. The company agreed to put No Name on a list, but warned me that the Conservatory would be demolished as soon as possible. So the board shifted its focus back to repairing the exterior of the Soap Factory. Meanwhile, Ryan's demolition of the Conservatory was delayed by protracted negotiations with two remaining mall tenants and difficulty finding anchor tenants for the proposed office tower. Those delays bought us time, several months in which deconstruction could be started in areas of the enormous retail complex far away from the spaces still occupied by tenants.

The Conservatory was still standing in early 1997 when I learned the Minnesota OEA was accepting grant applications to help private, public, and nonprofit organizations finance projects that "prevented pollution, reduced waste, or conserved resources." I believed our proposed recycling of materials from

the Conservatory achieved all three of these objectives, so I contacted the OEA.

The OEA's receptionist forwarded a report that not only quantified the waste likely to result from the Conservatory's demolition, but also verified that all of the items we believed could be reused at the Soap Factory would indeed be sent to landfills. Armed with this information, the No Name board decided it was worth calling Ryan again. This time, I was connected with Ryan's point-person for the OEA report. He seemed impressed that we had done our homework and scheduled a meeting to review the list of equipment and materials we needed to renovate the Soap Factory. At the end of the meeting, Ryan agreed to help us determine what could be saved, provided we used a licensed salvage crew for deconstruction for safety and insurance purposes.

We soon realized No Name needed additional input from building-industry professionals. Fred King, a member of our advisory committee, also sat on the board of directors for the Twin Cities chapter of the Association for Facilities Engineering (AFE). He suggested that we present our project at a monthly AFE meeting and ask for assistance from engineers and facility managers involved in designing, constructing, operating, and maintaining all types of buildings. The broad range of expertise contributed by AFE members and sponsors proved invaluable. Engineers from the mechanical and electrical firm that designed the original building systems for the Conservatory offered advice about what could be salvaged and safely reused. An AFE member, a licensed master electrician and former code official, helped us select specific electrical system components appropriate for future use of the Soap Factory.

Fortunately, the construction management division of an architectural firm located two blocks from the Soap Factory specialized in deconstruction and reuse. We invited the leader of this group to lunch and persuaded him to walk through the Conservatory with us to help figure out deconstruction techniques. From then on we let him know whenever we were touring the Conservatory, and he joined us. He remained "on call" to respond to our questions throughout the planning and deconstruction phases.

We also consulted with local code officials on health and safety matters. For example, we learned that for fire doors to maintain their established ratings, they had to be punched from the walls with their frames and assemblies intact. When there was ambivalence about whether we could reuse something and still meet current code requirements, we struck these from our list. Ryan and our advisors also encouraged us to salvage equipment we'd never considered, such as standard light fixtures, electrical panels, shelves, and mop sinks.

EXTERIOR VIEW OF THE CONSERVATORY IN 1987. PHOTO PROVIDED BY MICHAUD COOLEY ERICKSON.

The Conservatory had been solidly constructed of highly durable materials, and this meant that deconstruction often required shattering, ripping, and cutting items from their existing locations. When we first reviewed saving cast-iron benches located in the Conservatory's two atria, we were told their removal would require a crane because they were welded together. Later, Ryan's construction project manager figured out how to cut the benches apart efficiently, but it still took six burly volunteers to lift and carry each curved bench.

The Soap Factory required new tile in the bathrooms.

Although most of the ceramic tile installed in the Conservatory could not be saved, our architectural advisor and Ryan's project manager determined how to salvage some of the Italian marble tile. Because the marble had been sliced so thinly and adhered so firmly, removing it required shattering one piece and ripping remaining tiles off columns and walls. Just when we needed him, a local stone artist, who had attended a presentation where our project was discussed, volunteered to show us how to soak and scrape wall material from the back and deep-set the tile when we reused it.

Because of public concern about the vast amounts of marble and granite headed for local landfills, we wanted to save all we could. But the items we chose had to make practical sense for us, too. So when Ryan discovered boxes of unused ceramic tile in a Conservatory storage room a few months later, we reduced our total request for marble tile by an equivalent amount, choosing ease of reuse over the prestige and public interest in the finer finish materials. We tried to help find a home for the salvageable granite that was pin-hung to the Conservatory's exterior, but when we called the local tile association to see if anyone was interested,

VOLUNTEERS LESLIE WEST-
PHAL AND KEN POTTS USE A
WHEELBARROW TO TRANS-
PORT SALVAGED SIGNS.

OPPOSITE: LOCAL AFE MEM-

BERS NOT ONLY PROVIDED

THE TRUCKS NEEDED TO

TRANSPORT SALVAGED ITEMS,

BUT ALSO SENT EXPERIENCED

CREWS TO TRAIN SOAP FAC-

TORY VOLUNTEERS.

the answer was, "It's cheaper to buy new." When transportation, storage and refurbishment expenses are added to the labor costs of deconstructing and reusing materials and equipment, this conclusion proved true for most of the items salvaged and now installed at the Soap Factory. But this approach made economic sense for us for several reasons: the initial labor was donated, we had extremely limited funds to buy new materials and equipment and we had ample storage space (albeit unheated) on the top two floors of the Soap Factory. Ultimately, Ryan directed its own subcontractors to remove items and set them aside for us as part of their regular demolition work, rather than schedule separate site access for a special salvage crew, so we saved the cash expense of hiring our own crew.

ABOVE: INTERIOR OF THE

SOAP FACTORY BEFORE

RENOVATION ACTIVITIES

BEGAN.

Ryan notified us by letter that it tentatively agreed to deconstruct and donate items with a salvage value of $86,825 to No Name. This amount was based on values provided in the OEA report multiplied by the quantities of specific materials and equipment we'd requested. We sent this letter and our list of items to be salvaged to the OEA as part of our grant application, demonstrating that our contribution of materials would exceed the one-to-one match requirement up to the OEA's ceiling of $75,000.

Two months later, Ryan officially approved our project. As Ryan and its subcontractors were donating the labor cost of deconstructing materials, we assumed responsibility for transporting salvaged items from the Conservatory's loading dock two miles across town to the Soap Factory's riverfront site. Within a month, we developed a schedule and recruited enough volunteers for loading, unloading, storage and transportation tasks. We also secured trucks and driver sponsorships, which were made more complicated by the size limitations of the extremely small elevator that carried vehicles down to the Conservatory's underground loading dock.

REAR OF THE SOAP FACTORY (RED BRICK BUILDING ON RIGHT IN PHOTO BELOW) SEEN IN NEIGHBORHOOD CONTEXT OF HISTORIC PILLSBURY MILLS. THE RED TILE GRAIN ELEVATOR, LEFT, IS BEING CONVERTED INTO CONDOS OVERLOOKING THE MISSISSIPPI RIVER AND CENTRAL MINNEAPOLIS.

The local AFE Chapter helped us recruit sponsors who not only donated vehicles, fuel and drivers, but also, in some instances, sent staff who taught our volunteers how to load stake bed trucks and cube vans to the brim, then unpack them swiftly and efficiently.

We learned that the best way to engage the community was to simply tell our story and ask for help. Everyone seemed to be wondering what could be done to save pieces of the Conservatory. We'd spent the time figuring it out and could offer a sense of accomplishment to those willing to roll up their sleeves and work hard. University students, artists, architects, engineers, nearby residents, employees of local businesses, and others joined our volunteer corps after board members asked for help when they attended community or professional meetings or lectured at local campuses. For example, I was invited to present our project plan during the Landmark Series on Sustainable Development in St. Paul. At the end of our presentation, I told the standing-room-only crowd that if anyone was interested in putting words into action they should find me in the lobby after we adjourned. About a dozen people signed our volunteer sheet on the spot. Many others took information and called later to tell us how they could assist.

A few unexpected events were inevitable as deconstruction proceeded. On the first day that we were scheduled to move items off the Conservatory's loading dock, the sponsored truck and driver never showed up, leaving volunteers stranded at both the Conservatory and the Soap Factory. The dispatcher at the trucking company understood the situation and said, "I'll be right there." He found someone to cover for him, hopped in a cube van and filled in for the missing truck and driver.

During the transportation phase we also accepted the donation of materials left by others on the loading dock. This increased our logistical challenges. Saving two dozen large pieces of laminated glass once part of monumental light fixtures meant we needed a truck specifically designed to transport sheets of glass. Luckily, a friend of an AFE member owned a glass company, which was able to send a truck, a driver and several pairs of work gloves so volunteers could safely handle the glass.

On the final day of deconstruction, the elevator for transporting vehicles from street level to the loading dock broke down while we were packing a truck with salvaged items. This was the only vehicle left in the building, and I had visions

EXTERIOR VIEW OF THE SOAP FACTORY (2004). THE ORIGINAL THREE-STORY SECTION OF THE BUILDING (UPPER RIGHT) WAS CONSTRUCTED IN 1892. ALTHOUGH IT HAS BEEN EXPANDED TWICE, THE SOAP FACTORY REMAINS ON ITS ORIGINAL SITE NEAR ST. ANTHONY FALLS, THE BIRTHPLACE OF MINNEAPOLIS.

of trying to explain how we had saved tens of thousands of dollars worth of tile, lights, doors, sinks and other items but left a truck buried in the rubble. Ryan's construction supervisor then announced, "We think we can fix the elevator for one last run, but that's the last truck driving out of this building." Quickly, we called to turn back the other trucks en route.

AFE board member Jerry Hagen took charge and started shouting instructions over the din and through the dust created by crews that had already begun preparing for actual demolition in other areas of the building. We unloaded and reloaded our stake bed truck in record time, miraculously leaving less than a half-dozen items on the loading dock. There was only enough room to squeeze the driver into the front seat. The rest of us rode a passenger elevator up above ground.

Several months later, the OEA awarded No Name a $75,000 grant for the reuse of salvaged items. With the money, No Name hired architects and engineers to create floor plans and other drawings, as well as provide cost information needed to raise additional construction funds. Six years after deconstruction first began, we have installed salvaged sinks and countertops, ceramic tile, bathroom partitions, fire exit signs, electrical panels, light fixtures, fire doors, toilet paper holders, handicapped rails, paper towel dispensers with built-in wastepaper baskets, a baby-changing table, mirrors and a host of miscellaneous items at the Soap Factory. Four bathrooms have been renovated, doors throughout the first floor replaced, a security/fire-alarm system installed and major electrical system improvements completed.

No one who has worked on this project will ever view buildings the same way again. We now think about what goes on beneath the floors, above the ceilings and behind the walls——all the places where we replaced wiring, plumbing and other infrastructure to support what we had salvaged. We think about the origins and environmental impact of materials, equipment, and cleaning or refurbishment supplies.

While it often seems as though we cast a mere pebble into an ocean of possibilities, thousands of people have benefited from our efforts. Several hundred artists have shown their work so far and more than 20,000 people visited the Soap Factory during the renovation. Volunteers from the project have led other deconstruction efforts, including the salvage and reuse of stadium benches that otherwise would have been sent to a landfill when the street level of the Minneapolis Armory was converted to a parking garage.

Today, we are considering the best use for unoccupied areas of our building, which might become space for an experimental theater or a variety of other small, complementary arts groups or creative service firms. The relationships we built with our neighbors and the larger community during our renovation project have led to our participation on a task force currently reviewing two developers' plans to build on sites that share property lines with the Soap Factory. One plan is for several high-rise towers with 1,400 condominium units, the second plan is a low-rise complex of 52 condominium units. If done well, these developments will achieve the neighborhood's goal of increasing foot traffic and will bring audiences to our doorstep. In typical No Name fashion, we're now part of an ongoing multi-directional conversation between neighbors, developers and the city to build a new urban community from the remnants of other eras. ♥

OPENING NIGHT RECEPTION FOR THE "HOT HOUSE '04" GROUP EXHIBIT AT THE SOAP FACTORY, SPRING 2004.

building salvage resources

Architectural Salvage News
www.architecturalsalvagenews.com

Beyond Waste
www.beyondwaste.com

Building Materials Reuse Association
www.ubma.org

The Green Institute
www.greeninstitute.org

Institute for Local Self-Reliance
www.ilsr.org/recycling/index.html

Minnesota Sustainable Design Guide
www.sustainabledesignguide.umn.edu

Minnesota Environmental Initiative
www.mn-ei.org

Minnesota Materials Exchange
www.mnexchange.org

Minnesota Office of Environmental Assistance
www.moea.state.mn.us

The New Rules Project
www.newrules.org/environment/candd.html

Garden of Hope

Patients, doctors and community create a healing garden at a cancer clinic

CLARE COOPER MARCUS

Ann Chamberlain, artist and professor at the San Francisco Art Institute, was diagnosed with breast cancer in 1994. As she came for appointments and chemotherapy treatment at Mount Zion Clinical Cancer Center at the University of California-San Francisco, she was troubled by a concrete-paved courtyard that, except for a raised planter and a few mature trees, was unfurnished and unused. "Why isn't this a garden?" she asked her surgeon, Dr. Laura Esserman, who replied, "Why don't we make it into one?"

This was the start of a participatory process that soon took on its own momentum. Dr. Esserman raised funds for a redesign (she also holds an MBA degree), and Chamberlain brought seeds for chemotherapy patients to grow in paper cups and later plant out in the sparse areas of the courtyard that were not landscaped. Some brought plants from home to add to the environment. As people saw the potential for change, interest grew.

During 1995 and 1996, Chamberlain was awarded a residency at the hospital as an artist through the Haas Family Fund. She continued to work with patients, organizing tile-making workshops and events in the garden (for example, tai chi classes and a solstice ceremony) to demonstrate that this was a place where things could happen.

Katsy Swan, a garden designer who had created many gardens at Stanford Medical Center, was brought into the process. The three women made a powerful team: Chamberlain, the original instigator and organizer, understood the dynamics of the hospital community and knew the site well; Swan had extensive knowledge of appropriate plants and drew schematic designs for a garden that could serve many different users;

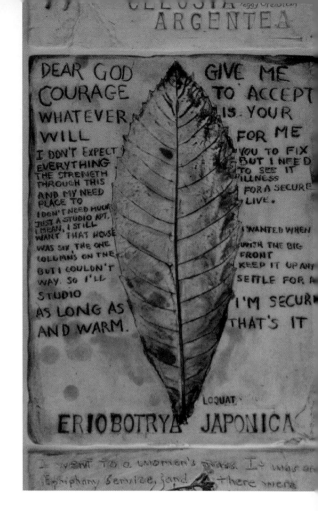

PATIENTS AND FAMILY MEMBERS EXPRESS THEIR DEEPEST THOUGHTS ON 525 HANDMADE TILES. THE TILES COVER THE INTERIOR WALL OF THE CORRIDOR THAT SKIRTS THE GARDEN.

NANDINA DOMESTICA

After chemotherapy
ended I dreamt that I
was in a war but the
enemy soldiers were gone
And I was afraid to put
down my gun because they might
be lurking somewhere, even though I was
looking on a beautiful landscape
which appeared calm.

I was worried:
had I won "the
war" was the
enemy gone;
could I go on
living without
the weapons of
chemotherapy?

SENECIO HYBRIDUS
CINERARIA

Dear God,

and Esserman knew how to draw in financial support and began to see the potential for redesigning this whole section of the cancer clinic around the emerging garden.

As the design process progressed, a workshop with patients and staff elicited ideas. They included requests for a variety of places to sit, a water element, lighting to extend use after dark, places to find privacy, baffles on a noisy air compressor and planting to shade a long interior corridor that felt like a furnace on summer afternoons.

The energy generated around the creation of the garden ignited a series of changes that resulted in the transformation of the entire wing of the medical center, known as the Ida and Joseph Friend Cancer Resource Center. The Center encompasses a library and resource center, rooms for exercise and yoga classes, offices for nutrition and spiritual counseling and a small cafe constructed to jut out into the garden and provide easy access for those who want to eat outdoors. The bow-fronted cafe is sited in the corner of the garden that catches the sun from midmorning to midafternoon.

The long glass-walled corridor forms the major circulation route for the resource center and defines the eastern edge of the garden. People walking to a class or appointment immediately see the garden—a not insignificant fact, since many hospital gardens are tucked away, and rarely

are there signs designating their presence. After spearheading the redesign of the garden, Chamberlain turned her attention to this corridor. "It was white and clinical and decorated with posters of lab technicians in white coats declaring 'We are going to eradicate cancer!' When Herb Caen [a much-loved local columnist] was being treated here for lung cancer, he dubbed it Dead Man Walking corridor! I wanted something that spoke of the subjective experiences of patients and doctors."

Working with ceramists Kenyon Lewis, Martha Heavenston and Cenri Nojima, Chamberlain started pressing leaves and flowers from the garden into 12- by 16-inch off-white tiles. Some years earlier Elaine Sedlack, senior horticulturalist at the University of California-Berkeley Botanic Garden, had collaborated with a Chinese herbalist on the installation of a garden of Asian specimens used in cancer treatment. Chamberlain used cuttings from these plants to imprint tiles at the entrance to the building, along with information about how the plants are used. Recently, practitioners of traditional medicine in China were contacted, and clinical trials are now underway on some of these herbs.

This tile-making activity developed into a number of workshops where cancer patients, cancer survivors, family members and friends created a total of 525 tiles that now cover the interior wall of the corridor for a length of 85 feet. "People need to know that their story matters. We wanted to make it impossible for those dreadful posters ever to be put up again!" Each tile has a leaf or flower impressed into it, the Latin name beneath it, and a personal poem, story or quotation inscribed by the tile-maker. The tiles not only provide a decorative and moving addition to an otherwise bland corridor, but also create a botanical element that brings the garden inside. From the garden, the wall appears as an attractive frieze, visible through the glass-walled corridor.

PARTICIPATING IN THE DESIGN OF THE GARDEN AND LEAVING A RECORD OF THEIR STORIES IN THE ADJACENT CORRIDOR GAVE PATIENTS AND STAFF A SENSE OF CONTROL. SUCH EMPOWERMENT HAS BEEN SHOWN TO REDUCE STRESS AND IMPROVE IMMUNE FUNCTIONING AND JOB SATISFACTION.

The constant change in the garden balances the permanence of the tiles. The stories on the tiles express love, fear, grief and faith, and reflect the emotions aroused at a time of medical crisis. The inscription on Ann's tile reads:

This year in the garden I learned to live with my eyes on the sky, to love the peachy pinkness of the pansy, to lie belly down on the warm cement as the wind picks up and watch the golden coreopsis dance and bob like exploding fireworks.
This year, I learned to live like a plant.

The tile-making workshops have been hugely popular with patients and staff who are thus able to tell their stories and contribute to the aesthetic environment of the Cancer Resource Center. When the Breast Care Center moved across the street, Esserman requested tile work for the new waiting room. Workshops were held weekly in the café next to the Healing Garden to produce many hundreds more tiles for the new facility.

Some people come into a hospital garden to seek distraction, to forget for a moment the gloomy prognosis they may just have heard or to gain some perspective before attending a difficult staff meeting. The garden at the Cancer Resource Center offers plentiful, subtle and soothing distractions: feathery shadows of podocarpus leaves on a gravel pathway, the late afternoon sun illuminating the corridor tiles, a hummingbird hovering to drink at the fountain, tendrils of a climbing wisteria moving in the breeze, a seagull circling high above, two men at a table deep in conversation. Many more people than those who actually enter the garden take enjoyment from its presence: People passing along the tiled corridor often turn their eyes towards the garden as they pass by, or stop briefly to look out at the greenery.

IN A HOSPITAL SETTING,
ART, SCULPTURE OR
OTHER HUMAN-MADE
ELEMENTS NEED TO BE
UNAMBIGUOUSLY POSI-
TIVE IN THEIR MESSAGE.
TILES AT THE HEALING
GARDEN THAT EXPRESSED
FEAR OR SADNESS WERE,
NONETHELESS, VIEWED AS
POSITIVE BECAUSE PEOPLE
HAD BEEN ENABLED TO
TELL THEIR OWN STORIES.

Esserman recalls, "One of my patients told me she always spent an hour in the garden before she came up to see me. She watched the garden change. Some flowers faded, others were just beginning, soon to be brilliant. It inspired her to believe that her illness may have its seasons too. To her, the garden was hope."

When the university moved the cancer center to a new, much larger facility in 2002, the building became home to an integrated Women's Health Center, which centralizes women's medical services and well-care. Now, the garden lends its tranquility to an entirely new group of patients, while remaining a treasured space for hospital staff. Meredithe Mendelsohn, the former administrator of the cancer center, considers it one of the best kept secrets in the neighborhood. "It's one of the few places where we can go and get a little break from it all."

The Healing Garden (for that is now its official designation) is what every hospital garden should be—a green oasis that offers as great a contrast as possible to the clinical human-made environment and often stressful atmosphere inside. Chamberlain, Swan and Esserman seized on the unfulfilled potential of a bleak, unused courtyard and transformed it into a remarkable place of beauty, restoration and healing. ♥

Adapted with permission from "Hospital Oasis," first published in *Landscape Architecture* magazine.

MURAL DETAIL: THE DESIGN WAS AUTHORED BY A BOY I HAD ASKED TO LEAVE THE ROOM WHEN HIS ACTING OUT BECAME TOO DISTRACTING TO EVERYONE ELSE. DISCIPLINE DIDN'T NEGATE GOOD WORK.

ALL PHOTOS IN THIS STORY BY KIKO DENZER.

Mud Murals

An Oregon school learns to color outside the lines

KIKO DENZER

Times were hard at Fairplay Middle School in Corvallis, Oregon. Despite having doubled up to share facilities with another school, the school was scheduled to shut down at the end of the year. Despite these conditions, School Principal Marla McVay intended to reinforce her students' self-image by

having them leave a lasting mark on the school building itself. Without knowing the precise nature of the project, she hired me for a two-week stint as artist-in-residence to propose and coordinate a project to help the children and community create a sense of place.

On my first visit, I met the "Fairplay Foresters," a name the students had acquired as a result of participating in a statewide 4-H program that had them planting trees around the school and working in gardens and greenhouses. Because Fairplay was the first 4-H school established in the state, an agricultural theme seemed appropriate. A new book I was carrying around, *African Painted Houses*, by Gary Van Wyk, inspired the format for the project. The book describes how Basotho women in South Africa annually redecorate their homes in colored earthen plasters incised with designs inspired by their lives, landscape, and traditions. The houses themselves, flat and low with few windows, rise up out of a spare, but starkly beautiful landscape. In this context, the murals become a stunning integration of culture and landscape.

Like so many other modern American schools, Fairplay is also flat and low, with many long, impersonal walls. And like the building, the educational landscape is equally stark. Classes are crowded, which is relieved by

bringing in a few "temporary" modular classrooms that are little more than plywood boxes with a few windows and a door. In this atmosphere, teachers devote tremendous time and energy to managing too many students. Fairplay is but one of many such schools in Oregon, which ranks 48th in the nation for its support for art in schools. Because funding for art and other "non-essential subjects" has been cut almost to zero, it is the PTA, not the school, that pays for artists-in-residence like me.

Despite the surrounding trees and green, Fairplay's buildings were pretty grim and institutional. Lifeless and ill-proportioned brick and masonry walls offered no decorative detail to bring the massive boxes down to a human scale (much less a child's scale). The most obvious failure was the entrance—a small double doorway set in the middle of a monotonous wall of red brick more than one hundred feet long, broken in several places by similar-looking doors and windows. There was no welcome, and nothing, even, to distinguish the front entrance—except two nondescript potted plants and a tiny wooden sign with the word "office," which was hard to spot under a dark soffit. During an introductory slide show, I asked the children how visitors might find their way in. The kids dutifully said there was a sign. Then I showed them a slide I'd taken of the entrance, the sign completely hidden by shade. Silence....

FAIRPLAY SCHOOL COURT-
YARD, BEFORE.
IN BASUTHO AFRICAN
CULTURE, THE ENTRANCE TO
A BUILDING IS TREATED AS
SACRED SPACE, SINCE THAT
IS WHERE THE DUTY OF HOS-
PITALITY IS CARRIED OUT.
IN AMERICA, HOWEVER,
VISITORS ARE LUCKY TO SEE
A POTTED PLANT OR TWO AT
THE DOORWAY.

The next slide was a Basotho house, decorated with a brilliant design that filled the flat walls and highlighted the doorway. Children filled the room with "oohs" and "aaahs." So I proposed that the kids develop their own designs, based on their own experience of nature and the plant life around them, which we would incorporate into a mural to make the blank school walls come to life. I explained the idea with slides of Basotho houses and shared close-up photos of the natural design of plants.

We spent our first sessions drawing plant leaves and flowers, and using those drawings to make strong, simple designs. Working from the Basotho example, I asked kids to make mirror images of their designs, working in squares around a common center. We folded paper in four or eight equal rectangles; kids drew a design in a single rectangle with a soft lead pencil, folded the paper, rubbed the back, and transferred a mirror image onto the next rectangle. We repeated the process until each person had a beautiful design based on four to eight duplicates of their pattern, each duplicate mirroring the one before.

For mud practice, and so that everyone could make an individual piece to take home, we all reproduced a plant pattern in mud on a twelve-inch square backing sheet of gypsum

FAIRPLAY SCHOOL COURT-
YARD, AFTER.
THE REGULAR, RHYTHMIC
PATTERN OF THE MURAL
DIRECTS VISITORS TO THE
ENTRANCE. THESE GEOMET-
RIC DIVISIONS BREAK LARGE
ARCHITECTURAL FORMS
INTO MORE INVITING
HUMAN SCALE.

wallboard. Then we selected an arrangement of designs that would fit the wall space and frame the school's entry. McVay was as enthusiastic as the kids about the idea of covering the walls with colored mud; she had immediately connected with the beauty and power of the African example.

We finished the project in three days, working with small teams of students from different classrooms. Because we were short on time, we had to skip one of the best parts of the process, where the students get to take off their shoes and mix the mud barefoot. But slathering the pre-mixed mud on the walls was almost as good as barefoot stomping. We threw handfuls onto the walls and then smoothed them out with trowels. When we had a nice flat surface, we drew out the patterns, one square at a time, and then applied pigments made of local clays mixed with water.

As a final protective measure, after the mud was dry, I sprayed it with a solution of sodium silicate (waterglass) and water, which binds the material so that rain and even running water won't wear it away. In Basotholand, they have another approach to saving murals: they make new ones every year. ♥

how to make a mud mural

KIKO DENZER

MOST OF THE WORLD'S PEOPLE use earth to make their homes; it is the most common building material on the planet. For comfort, beauty, ease of construction, ecology and economy, it beats cement, hands down.

I generally make mud with what's underfoot. I can usually find clay subsoil close by, with which I mix approximately 3–4 parts sand and as much water and fiber (in that order) as is best for whatever application I need.

Clay binds the sand (as Portland cement binds aggregate). Fiber, in the form of straw or manure, adds tensile strength and plasticity. I use short fiber for detail work and thin mural plasters. Cow manure is uniformly short and finer than horse manure because it goes through more stomachs, but with squeamish groups or places where liability and health codes are at issue, I substitute chopped straw, paper pulp, cattail fluff, etc. (Longer straw is best for free-standing sculptural work where you need wet mud to stay where you put it. Very wet, straw-rich mixes are best for speed and wet strength; stiffer mixes can be better for surface modeling.)

Mud sticks well to most surfaces; texture helps, but isn't always necessary. Sometimes a finer mud will work better on a smoother surface. Mud sticks well to wood, but because the two materials respond differently to moisture, wood is generally treated as for stucco with a layer of tarpaper, followed by expanded metal lath, or

anything else with texture to it. I have applied mud directly to masonry, masonite and sheetrock with good success.

For the murals, I may add cooked wheat paste (available commercially as [non-vinyl] wallpaper paste, or homemade by pouring a thin batter of flour and water into an equal volume of boiling water)—about a cup or two of paste for a wheelbarrow full of mix—but I go more by feel than by exact measure, stopping when the mud goes from feeling sandy and loose to "fatty" and cohesive.

I collect natural earthen pigments when I see them in road cuts or construction sites. All the colors for the Fairplay mural (yellow, red and black) were local clays. However, in a pinch, concrete pigments work well (Davis Colors, for example, tend to be various oxides of iron, from bright yellow to black, and quite potent in small amounts. Beware blues and greens, however, some of which can be made from toxic heavy metals—ask to see Material Safety Data Sheets when considering unfamiliar pigments).

There are a few rules common to mud, cement and stucco. Too much sand makes a weak mix. Too much clay (or cement) causes shrinkage and cracking. It's always good to make a few test mixes and try them out before you commit yourself to many square feet.

A 50/50 solution of sodium silicate (waterglass) and water sprayed or brushed onto completely dry mud and allowed to dry again slowly will cement the material so well that a hose held on it won't have noticeable effect. When brushed on, it does tend to darken colors. I buy it in bulk from a ceramic supply house. Waterglass has been a recent discovery for me, one that makes murals possible in less protected areas where I might not have risked it before. But the best way to preserve art is simply to keep making it anew!

mud mural and earth building resources

BOOKS

African Canvas: The Art of West African Women. Margaret Courtney-Clarke, Maya Angelou. (New York: Rizzoli, 1990). Photo essay of colorfully patterned West African mud homes and pottery.

African Painted Houses: Basotho Dwellings in Southern Africa. Gary Van Wyk. (New York: Harry Abrams, 1998). Basotho women paint brilliant geometric murals on the plaster walls of their houses. The book documents this beautiful art and explores the political message much of the art carries.

Architecture for the Poor: An Experiment in Rural Egypt. Hassan Fathy. (Chicago: University of Chicago Press, 2000). This classic describes building the village of New Gourna, near Luxor, Egypt, without the use of modern and expensive materials such as steel and concrete.

Build Your Own Earth Oven: A Low-Cost, Wood-Fired, Mud Oven; Simple Sourdough Bread, Perfect Loaves. Kiko Denzer. (Blodgett, OR: Hand Print Press, 2000). Illustrated handbook for making a wood-fired oven out of hand-formed earth, as well as the authentic, naturally-leavened hearth breads to bake in it. The book is also a popular primer on the technique of "cob" construction, as the earthen-building tradition is known in Britain.

The Cobber's Companion: How to Build Your Own Earthen Home. Michael Smith. (Cottage Grove, OR: COB Cottage Co., 1998). Topics in this how-to include building with earth, sand and straw as well as selecting building materials and reducing dependency on eco-unfriendly practices.

Community Murals Handbook & Case Studies. A Rural Action Community Toolbox Book, Amy Lipka and Steven McDaniel. (Rural Action's Arts & Cultural Heritage Program, Trimble OH, 2001). Covers community involvement, publicity, technical information, volunteers, safety & liability, costs, funding, marketing and more.

Dig Your Hands in the Dirt: A Manual for Making Art Out of Earth. Kiko Denzer. (Blodgett, OR: Hand Print Press, 2005). A primer for making murals, labyrinths, sundials and other environmental sculpture projects. Includes photos, illustrations, step-by-step instructions for working with earth.

Drawing with Children: A Creative Method for Adult Beginners, Too. Mona Brookes. (New York: JP Tracher, 1996). Designed for parents and teachers of children of all ages, this book presents easy-to-follow lessons for developing artistic skill and for using drawing in other scholastic subjects.

The Hand-Sculpted House: A Philosophical and Practical Guide to Building a Cob Cottage. Ianto Evans, et. al. (South Burlington, VT: Chelsea Green, 2002). Arguably the most comprehensive book on cob construction methods available.

Spectacular Vernacular: The Adobe Tradition. Jean-Louis Bourgeois and Carollee Pelos. (Aperture Foundation, 1989, 1996). Sumptuous color tour of earthen buildings, especially of West Africa and Southwestern Asia.

WORKSHOP PROVIDERS

Cob Cottage Company, www.cobcottage.com
Cobworks, www.cobworks.com
Groundworks, www.cpros.com/~sequoia

CELEBRATING CULTURE

An Artist Journeys Home

ANNIE RACHELE LANZILLOTTO

Go home. Work with the mentalities you fled in your development. Wrestle your neighbors. Call out your ancestors.

I gave myself this challenge and although the journey home was arduous, it's one I recommend. My story begins at my mother's stove, her aluminum pot of water boiling. *Sopre il forno caldo* – over the hot stove; the woman over the fire, tending to the food. Here is a hot spot, an open channel to all the world's spirit. She was making me a pasta for my birthday. She threw one bag of *penne* into the boiling water when there was a pounding knock at the door. Instinctively she grabbed a second bag, ripped it open for whoever was at the door surely would stay and eat, and as she tossed the pasta into the water she yelled my name and fell backwards into my arms. Her back was soaking wet. In that moment an aneurysm had split the wall of her ascending aorta. When she said, "I am fine. I just need to lay on the couch," we knew that something was mortally wrong. Within hours she was in the O.R., her heart beating open in the surgical air. After the repair, a post-op staff infection gutted her sternum, creating an open chest wound the mass of a banana. Six weeks later she was off oxygen. Armed with jugs of sterile water, surgical gloves and bandages, face masks, tongue depressors and a tub of Silverdene (designed to promote new skin growth for burn victims), I drove my mother slowly home in a used Pontiac lemon that I'd bought with all we'd had just for this momentous escort, my mother's return into fresh air to her home. Six months into her recuperation, I said, "Ma, today's the day. We're going out. No doctors' appointments, just out! Whereva ya wanna go…." I expected her to say let's go to the water, let's see something beautiful. Her response shocked me, and changed my life and career.

"Arthur Avenue. Let's go to The Market." Yes, she chose the Bronx where we all grew up, the Bronx where all our relatives this side of the Atlantic were buried, the Bronx where we all had traumatized youths, the Bronx: our collective hearts' home. She reapplied her Pink Lightning lipstick and made the decision to leave the wheelchair in the trunk of the car for the first time. When I opened the door to the Arthur Avenue Retail Market she came alive in a way I had never seen. She was sixteen again; it could have been 1943 as she ambled amongst stacks of peppers, tasting from the grapes and open barrels of olives, and small hunks of *parmigiano reggiano*. She gained an edge in her attitude. She pointed at hanging *provolones*. She folded sprigs of parsley like money into her pocketbook. She was back. Enter Rachele Pettruzzelli Lanzillotto, an Italian-American Bronx woman who, though just getting on her feet, unearthed the power of how to interact, bargain, flirt, argue, sparkle, steal. She walked to the back of the market to Mike's Deli where she recognized the man behind the counter, Mike, the proprietor. They had interacted across that counter intermittently for over fifty years; he as a merchant, she as a shopper. He leaned over the counter, a military portrait of El Duce on the wall between the hanging salamis behind him, and as if no time had passed he handed her a slice of *soppressata*, singing *ciao bella* with elongated "L" sounds. For my mother, his slice of *soppressata* had the memory-prodding magic of Proust's madeleine. *Soppressata* was definitely not part of her strict keep-the-blood-pressure-low-to-stay-alive no-salt diet, yet she accepted the slice, put it on her tongue, and a rush of stories followed: memories of the chanting Bronx pushcart peddlers of her youth, how her father had once had an ice route on Arthur Avenue, her mother Rose's knack for picking live spring chickens to roast and soup chickens for soup, grand statues from the feasts for Our Lady of Monte Carmelo. Here was a woman who had lived through the trauma of a near-death whammo! vascular catastrophe, had quit cigarettes and fatty meats in the matter of a day, and boom! the moment she steps foot on Arthur Avenue she is sucking on a slice of fat-speckled salami. It had taken us months to clear her lungs, weeks on a respirator. Now she was going to start her old arterially compromising habits again the first day she was out?

"Only here," she reassured me, "I'd never eat it anywhere else." What was going on here? And she wasn't the only one. As she chatted with other shoppers, soon there were three of them, all who had the familiar paper tape crosshatch on their sternums peeking out of their V-neck shirts gripping the scars from their recent bypass surgeries and valve replacements. They were here to do their walking in The Market, their *passeggiata*, to feel alive; sampling life at Mike's Deli with childish smiles. What magic and trust was transmitted over these countertops? What faith? I watched the way the merchants and shoppers leaned over, creating a vital intimacy; the countertops morphed into confessionals, into stages. People were interacting! The Market was alive for me in a way that theater had ceased to be. We went back several times and the visions and stories simmered within me. I was touched with the spirit of the pushcart peddler. Years later this would manifest as performance.

After a year of caretaking my mom, I shaved my head and headed downtown to recreate my life. I found a job, a lover, a sublet and a shrink. I performed my first solo theater piece, "Confessions of a Bronx Tomboy," based on her near death. Next followed a series of works that drew on The Market imagery. "Pocketing Garlic," commissioned by Franklin Furnace, opened with a chorus of garlic peddlers, and was centered around the act of my mother and grandmother tucking garlic and parsley in their pockets, refusing to pay money for what was essential to life. Then Dancing in the Streets put out a call for artists to create "site-specific community-based performance" in New York City. Here was my chance to heighten the daily drama of The Market by adding a layer of performance art.

I researched the late 1930s, when New York City Mayor Fiorello La Guardia built over one hundred city markets to get the immigrant pushcart peddlers off the streets in time for the World's Fair. He outlawed hawking and squawking, put a roof over their heads and dubbed the peddlers "merchants." Fifty-odd years later, three of these markets still functioned, selling food. I set out to bring "hawking and squawking" back through performance, and create what I heard as the street opera of pushcart peddling. The project was awarded a grant for research and development. The first thing I did was return to The Market with photographer Andrew Perret, buy two cappuccinos at Café al Mercato and hang out. I needed to observe and be observed. By my second visit the merchants knew what I would order. I watched and listened and got my toes wet in the fine art of Bronx interaction. The Market was an indoor piazza. I climbed back into my Bronx skin and my southern Italian heart. Dramatic interaction was the order of the day.

MARIO RIBAUDO OF MARIO'S MEAT MARKET SERENADING WHILE COOKING LAMB HEARTS. IN CROWD WITH MICROPHONE IS SINGER BRENDA CUMMINGS WITH LOCAL RESIDENT SHOPPER IDA CAROZZA. PHOTO BY ANDREW PERRET.

I bought another cappuccino and asked how one rents a stall in the market. The arts grant gave me the opportunity to be on equal footing with the merchants by renting "space" in "time." I went to the butcher counter and had my first of many talks with Mike Rella, the president of The Market, right over his counter. Rella had a passion for the history of The Market. He rented me a vacant fruit stand seventeen feet wide for three dollars per foot per week. Acrobats, opera singers, jugglers, painters, performance artists of all stripes gravitated to this chance to perform with people amongst fruits and vegetables with the pounding of meat cleavers echoing through their work. A baby grand piano was lent to the project, and I had it trucked up and tuned on site. Just hearing a piano being tuned amidst the gorgeous pyramids of shiny red peppers, yellow onions, the peeling papyrus-like white garlic was moving. "The Opera Stand" was born.

PHOTO BY ANDREW PERRET.

We got to work. I staged my Grandma Rose to demonstrate how to make the *cavateel*. She was ninety-six and no one was as adept at shaping the pasta and flipping the nascent *cavateel* off their fingertips. Her fingers were grasshoppers. Artist Audrey Kindred began to collect the outer layer of onion skins the merchants peeled and threw away to keep their onions looking young and fresh on the stands. She developed a technique of making masks by feathering red and yellow onion and white garlic skins. This stirred curiosity from the shoppers, some of whom would join her. Mike's Deli and Peter's Meat Market offered free plates of *provolone* and *mozzarella* and olives and finger sandwiches for passers-by. The senior shoppers from Mount Carmel Senior Center on 186th Street parked their pushcarts at our stand and started singing, and the gorgeous conflicts began. One fruit merchant blasted his radio once shoppers started singing. My aesthetic was to embrace the cacophony as an expression of pluralism, in fact to find drama there. When butcher Mario Ribaudo belted tenor arias, the other butchers pounded their cleavers saying the singing was going to his head and he better keep his mind on his work. Despite some resentments at the change we were imposing as outsiders to the community, distrust because we weren't "selling" anything, and the fact that our crowds were clogging the aisles and blocking their regular shoppers from getting to their stands, the merchants voted a few weeks later to give us the space for the piano rent free. As our initial funding was running out, this was a boon. We had a core

following of senior shoppers who would await our arrival every Saturday. Here they sung out loud in the place they had shopped their whole lives. Ninety-six-year-old shoppers sang together with merchants and downtown artists. It was this trio formation that inspired me.

I began to instigate interactions as a practice and thought of myself as an Interaction Practitioner; directing trios of merchants, shoppers, and invited artists into scenarios. I would ask the artist to react to the scenario in such a way as to keep the ball in the air, keep the dramatic momentum moving, keep everybody physically safe and spiritually engaged. The artist's role was to instigate, to listen, to ignite performance, to provide a microphone for merchants and shoppers, to bring the scenarios to a level of dramatic intensity. We were guests in a workplace where families had spent decades, in some cases, generations. Cultivating a respect for that fact among my cast and crew was primary, and not without incident. We attended weekly merchants' meetings, traveled with merchants on their four a.m. shopping treks to the Hunts Point Cooperative Market, the New York City Terminal Produce Market and the Bronx Terminal Market. We became audience to the merchants' daily routines, and cultural investigators in the history of their lives. Arts grants followed. Commissioning funds from Dancing in the Streets and a Rockefeller Foundation Multi-Arts Production Grant and support from the Puffin Foundation allowed us the autonomy to create.

In instigating scenarios and arguments from the fabric of oral history and daily life, I called upon my own grandiose absurdities, magnifying the visions I perceived in the community after listening to many stories for over a year. Scenarios and short scripted arguments were inspired by direct observation and interviews. My method was to

MARIO RIBAUDO OF MARIO'S MEAT MARKET. PHOTO BY ANYA HITZENBERGER.

load the environment in ways that provoked drama. Through experimentation I learned performance facts I could count on during a show. I felt like a scientist experimenting with phototropism; I could load the environment with events that would naturally cause reactions in the organism. The Market was alive. The sound of a balloon popping would cause the butchers to pound their cleavers and shout a deep abdominal "Oh!"; the presence of period photographs of the neighborhood gave the diaspora of old timers who made pilgrimages to The Market a catalyst for memories of old stories and songs;

a free platter of sharp *provolone* would gather a crowd in one place faster than any other technique of arranging and moving groups of people; placing theatrical seating in front of the butcher counter gave the message clearly to watch transactions as drama; a checkered strip of linoleum dance floor rolled out between the fruit aisles gave shoppers a runway to dance on while they shopped. Although inspired by history and drawing on centuries of marketplace theater, my priority was to dream and create surreal images: installations of text on wood slats which otherwise showed food prices;

text on garlic; text on eggs; installation of a giant pocketbook with parsley and text sprouting out of it; video meditations of Grandma's peasant technique of breaking eggs; collages of images from merchant families' lives on hand trucks, née altars; luminary pushcarts expressing the shopper's fancy feeling of the *passeggiata*; getting dressed up to promenade; a Venetian-style

gondola on wheels to transport a revered elderly mandolin/accordion/guitar band up and down the fruit and vegetable aisles; a balcony above the crowd to provoke speeches from the merchants; the slow dance of passing heavy watermelons from dancer to shopper to dancer to shopper clear across the market to where they were cut and served.

Marketplace productions happened during regular business hours. Our scenarios were interruptions in the routine flow of shopping. For three winters from 1996 to 1998 we performed "How to Cook a Heart" on Valentine's Day. This grew from the daily rhythm of butcher Mario Ribaudo of Mario's Meat Market's business day that included a dormant period where he would rest his head on his counter. After many talks with Mario, tapping into his dilemmas, nostalgia, dreams and desires, I invited trapeze artist Tanya Gagné to come up to the Bronx and work with him. Ribaudo taught Gagné how to clean tripe. We cut a pipe over Mario's counter to make room for Gagné's trapeze bar. Gagné designed a series of strong warrior poses on his countertop and trapeze moves hovering over his stand. Gagné's stunning solo work over Mario's butcher case full of offal—intestines, tripe, Sicilian peasant specialties such as *fegatini, schemeral* (intestines wrapped around spleen stuffed with cheese and parsley) and of course hearts, heads, tongues, livers and bull penises—accompanied Ribaudo's singing and cooking. I set up an electric frying pan, spotlight and microphone atop Ribaudo's counter for him to cook his lamb hearts and sing tenor arias and peasant ballads. Gagné stunned The Market into silence, the cash registers ceased to ring for seven minutes, as merchants came out from behind their stands to see her mount her trapeze bar over the meat counter. The Market had the hush of a cathedral. This was a profound experience, drawing merchant and performer together in a surreal dream. To me, the fact that art could silence cash registers and add pause to the day was grand and stood in stark relief to everything the merchant families had worked for.

When I brought an artist into The Market, I brought the total artist, not just their performative selves, but their whole humanity. I was careful in bringing women into this male workplace. Gagné created a costume that covered her body yet showed her strength, drawing on the lines and colors in the lamb hearts Ribaudo sold. Other female dancers were uncomfortable working in this culture where bikini pin-ups alongside pictures of cuts of meat adorned butchers' back

TANYA GAGNÉ ON MARIO
RIBAUDO'S COUNTERTOP.
PHOTO BY ANDREW PERRET.

PERFORMANCE ARTIST PENNY
ARCADE AND MERCHANT
GIUSEPPE LIBERATORE
ON THE BALCONY TELLING
LIFE STORIES AND CALLING
THE NAMES OF FOODS. PHO-
TO BY ANYA HITZENBERGER.

freezers. As a strategy to literally bring this "to light" I asked Rella if we could enhance the images by hanging lights over the meat freezer and collaging bigger and bolder images of meat cuts interspersed with women's bodies. We ripped the pin-ups so illustrations of meat cuts shone through the images of women, thus magnifying the message of the butchers' freezer collages. Then we walked audiences through the rear freezer section to acknowledge it, bring it out of the shadows.

I wrote short scripts based on market oral histories. We played behind the counters, in the aisles, on top of the freezers, in the streets and on neighbors' balconies. I played Ribaudo's wife arguing with him about why he refused to teach the butchering business to one of his three daughters. Acrobat Hope Clark worked with *mozzarella* maker David Greco, creating ways to stretch a bridge of freshly made mozzarella fourteen feet long over the aisle of shoppers while Clark hung upside-down from the building's steel beams and pipes. I also set Clark in the neighborhood park a few blocks away. Again, our methodology was for her to hang out there; she began to swing on the bars and do handstands. People of all ages gravitated to her to watch and she expertly invited them to join her, creating gymnastic classes in the park. This work grew into a performance and procession that gave local children, who were not from families that traditionally shopped in the market, a way into the market. On production day, the children carried pumpkins down the block in procession behind me—I was playing the Ghost of the Pushcart Peddler, named "Chimaroot" (fingers like ginger root). Barefoot with a rickety wooden pushcart, I led the crowd into the market through the garbage garage turned photo gallery. Thanks to Materials for the Arts, who provided black velvet stage wings, we hung Andrew Perret's and Anya Hitzenberger's photos of our works and process on the red brick garage walls.

As much as we brought the theater community to The Market, we also brought The Market to the theater, when artists commissioned by Dancing in the Streets were invited to perform at The Guggenheim's Works & Process series. This exchange helped merge our worlds and gave a professional artist's context to the work. I created a cast of twenty, including

LOCAL YOUTH PUMPKIN PROCESSION FROM D'AURIA MURPHY SQUARE, DOWN HUGHES AVENUE, INTO THE ARTHUR AVENUE RETAIL MARKET. PHOTO BY ANYA HITZENBERGER.

merchants, shoppers and artists to recreate the market in the Guggenheim. Ribaudo wore his bloodiest butcher's apron, underdressed in a tuxedo for his transformation scene from butcher to tenor. Grandma Rose had her stage debut at ninety-six years old. She played the Garlic Queen, dressed as she asked to be, in a wedding gown and garlic headdress, playing the oldest shopper in the market and improvising what she does best, haggling with the merchants over the prices of food.

On Mothers Day 1997, we created a spring performance entitled, "Mammamia! You'll Never Get a Straight Answer Again!" In the fall we culminated our works with "*a'Schapett!*" (wiping the plate clean with the heel of the bread and savoring the end of the meal). That's what I was doing, savoring the juices of what was left of the culture I'd been steeped in. After the project's funding ended, we worked for the local business

ANNIE LANZILLOTTO, ARTIST VALERIE STRIAR. PHOTO BY ANYA HITZENBERGER.

association organizing street festivals and continuing to bring art into The Market and other local businesses. The merchants called us to join them in various events, from morning news features to the pivotal day when the first fast food restaurant was opened on Arthur Avenue. We came up and added drama to the locals who were protesting—I organized the chant "Viva Broccoli Rabe!" I had learned to believe in food, to believe that, as Audrey Kindred put it best, "When you eat the food of your ancestors, all the blood comes rushing down through the ages." ♥

ANNIE LANZILLOTTO AS "CHIMAROOT" THE PUSH-CART PEDDLER, CALLING UP TO HUGHES AVENUE RESIDENT PUPPETTA'S BALCONY, WHERE GUITARIST CHRIS CARBONE SERENADES. PHOTO BY ANYA HITZENBERGER.

"THE POWER OF UNITY" QUILT IS BASED ON THE BAHA'I FAITH'S CENTRAL TENET OF UNITY: THE UNITY OF ALL RACES, NATIONS AND RELIGIONS. THE QUILT WAS CREATED THROUGH CONSENSUS BY WOMEN FROM DIFFERENT RACIAL, CULTURAL AND FAITH BACKGROUNDS, INCLUDING MUSLIM, CHRISTIAN, JEWISH, CATHOLIC, BRITISH, CAUCASIAN AND AFRICAN-AMERICAN WOMEN.

Piecing a Bigger Story

Faith and the art of quilt-making

KATE MADDEN YEE

"Most of us think we have to travel thousands of miles to engage with people who think in radically different ways," says Clara Wainwright, a Boston-based public celebration artist, quilt maker and founder of the Faith Quilts Project, a collaborative effort that brings people together to talk about faith. "But I've always believed that they're right in your own neighborhood."

Americans experienced this principle in a violent and painful manner on September 11, 2001. Suddenly, it became clear that understanding faith and its manifestations was crucial to our collective welfare.

A year after the attacks, Wainwright saw PBS's program Frontline: "Faith and Doubt at Ground Zero," which explores how people's faith was challenged by the September 11th experience. Fascinated with the questions the program posed, such as how we understand good and evil and how we cope with human frailty, she embarked on a particular faith quest of her own. She decided to examine faith by making quilts with people from different traditions.

For Wainwright, quilt-making offers a form of consensus-building. "Historically, quilting has been very individual in terms of design," she says. "It's the piecing that has typically had a communal aspect. I saw an opportunity to use quilting more collaboratively, allowing new and experienced quilters to create the design together." Since she began quilting in 1971, Wainwright has created some forty fabric collages and quilts, some as solo projects, but mostly as collaborations.

During her thirty-plus years as a citizen artist, she developed deep links with the community. (Wainwright helped to establish the Boston Kite Festival and First Night, an alternative, arts-based New Year's Eve celebration that has launched over two hundred similar celebrations around the world.)

Drawing on her community connections, Wainwright began what became the Faith Quilts Project in October 2002. She set aside three years to explore the concept of faith,

RIGHT: "TREE OF FAITH" BY ISLAMIC CENTER OF BOSTON, WAYLAND, MASSACHUSETTS. PHOTO BY RICHARD HOWARD.

BELOW: CHILDREN'S QUILT. PHOTO COURTESY MASJID AL QUR'AN.

...WE IN THE FIRST WORLD CANNOT CONTINUE TO ISOLA...

dedicating that time to making quilts with people of different faiths. Via a contact at the Massachusetts College of Art, Wainwright met Palestinian, Indonesian and Pakistani women who attended Wayland Mosque in Wayland, Massachusetts. For nine weeks, Wainwright helped the women create a quilt that would represent their faith. From there, her contacts grew, her original three-year commitment expanded into four, and the intended twelve quilts mushroomed into more than fifty.

The quilts represent some two-dozen faith traditions, including Baha'i, African-American Muslim, Southeast Asian Muslim, Jewish, Catholic, Unitarian Universalist, Hindu, Native American, Mormon, Church of Scientology, Wiccan, Buddhist, Zoroastrian, Seventh Day Adventist, Episcopalian, Baptist and Methodist. Although a few quilts are the result of interfaith collaboration, most have been created within particular faith communities.

A year into the project, Wainwright recruited a team to help administer the expanding work. The staff includes a dialogue consultant, a director of development and exhibitions, a performance director, a project director, a public relations consultant and an advisory council chair. Wainwright also engaged more than thirty lead quilters. Supported by donations

SECTION OF BOSTON PUBLIC
LIBRARY'S "WE BOSTONIANS:
INTERSECTING SPIRITUAL
JOURNEY" QUILT ONE, MADE
BY SIXTY-SEVEN COLLABORA-
TIVE QUILTERS LED BY CLARA
WAINWRIGHT.

ALTHOUGH MOST OF THE
PARTICIPANTS HAD NEVER
WORKED WITH FABRIC AND
QUILTS, THEY OVERCAME
THEIR APPREHENSIONS AND
CUT AND ARRANGED FABRICS
TO CREATE SELF-PORTRAITS.

"WE BOSTONIANS" QUILT TWO
ON NEXT DOUBLE SPREAD.
QUILT PHOTOS BY RICHARD
HOWARD.

from private individuals and organizations, the Project operates under the auspices of the Public Conversations Project in Watertown, Massachusetts, a group that uses dialogue to resolve public disputes.

The Project's staff now includes Maggie Herzig, dialogue consultant and founding member of the Public Conversations Project, under which Faith Quilts operates financially; Mary Downes, executive director; and Reverend Katie Lee Crane (Unitarian Universalist), advisory council chair and more than twenty lead quilters. As Wainwright envisioned, the Project has proven rich in opportunities for conversation.

"Often what people learn in school about faith tradi-tions are theological principles, and what they read in the paper are accounts of bad behavior," Herzig says. "The process of making the quilts provides a combination of reflection, verbal exchange and the creation of something visually expressive. It invites people to talk about how faith shows up in their hearts and lives, and to speak about the value of faith, rather than focusing on what a faith institution does right or wrong."

After Wainwright has connected with a potential Faith Quilts group, she assigns a lead quilter to help the group develop its vision for communicating an idea of faith with the quilt. Lead quilters use verbal or writing exercises to help participants explore the shape of their faith. The lead quilter also helps the group with logistics, from how often to meet to what kind and color of fabric to use. Often participants con-tribute cloth that carries special meaning: A Turkish Muslim quilt contains fabric from Istanbul, fabric from Africa makes

WE USED TO THINK THAT SCIENCE WOULD...

DINNER AT THE SAME · KAREN ARMSTRONG · THE SPIRAL STAIRCASE 2004

up an African-American Muslim quilt, and the Monastery of St. Clare's quilt includes cloth once used to make habits.

As an initial exercise, Faith Quilters create a self-portrait out of cloth, which helps them to connect not only with the medium of quilting, but also with their own creativity. Then the group creates a fabric mandala as an exercise in working together.

"Most of the people I make quilts with are not quilters, and don't consider themselves artistic," Wainwright says. "But once they've made a self-portrait out of fabric and can see that the portraits have some resemblance, they begin to relax. The mandalas often become the center of the group's quilt. In a short fifteen- or twenty-minute exercise, people see that they can make a work of art together that has balance and beauty."

Each quilt is unique, yet many share similar symbols and features, a testament to the underlying commonality that is revealed when people gather to talk about faith. Rays of fabric spiral out from the center of some of the quilts; many have images from the natural world, such as light, fire, trees or birds.

SUFIA HASAN AND CLARA WAINWRIGHT. THE QUILT "OUR PATHWAYS TO ISLAM" IS THE RESULT OF THE COLLABORATION OF TWELVE AFRICAN-AMERICAN MUSLIM WOMEN FROM THREE BOSTON MASAJID (MUSLIM HOUSES OF WORSHIP)—MASJIDU LI HAMDILLAH, MASJID AL QUR'AN AND MASJID AN-NUR.

Diana Miller runs the Boston Alzheimer's Center and its Rogerson House Day Program and Assisted Living Program. After working on a quilt for her own faith community, Arlington Street Church in Boston, a Unitarian Universalist congregation, she began an interfaith quilt with eleven members of the Center in 2003, inviting participation from their caregivers and families as well. The quilt, entitled "We Remember," consists of fabric

squares with each of the program members' words about faith printed on them. Self-portraits of their caregivers act as a border to represent the community required to support people with the disease.

Another project drew twenty-six core participants from Temple Beth Zion in Brookline, Massachusetts, an independent Jewish community with more than six hundred congregants. These faith quilters, ranging in age from eight to ninety-one, gathered to work on two eight- by fourteen-foot quilts for more than a year. Each person developed ideas for a square that addresses a personally meaningful theme related to being Jewish, helped choose fabrics and created their images on their particular squares.

The project has deepened the community's connection, says Beverly Sky, creative director of the quilt group along with Meredith Joy, the organizational director.

"We took ten months to talk about design," Sky says. "Since we started, people have come and gone, but at least

CENTRAL MANDALA OF "WE BOSTONIANS" QUILT ONE, CREATED BY A DIVERSE GROUP—
A YOUNG HINDU, A YOUNG MUSLIM, A MIDDLE-AGED CATHOLIC TURNED UNITARIAN, A
MIDDLE-AGED JEW, A YOUNG SUFI, A CHINESE-AMERICAN AGNOSTIC, A SEEKER AND A
BUDDHIST. EACH PERSON CUT OUT MULTIPLE IDENTICAL SHAPES AND PLACED THEM IN
SYMMETRY, RESULTING IN THIS COLLABORATIVE IMAGE OF TRANSCENDENCE. PHOTO BY
RICHARD HOWARD.

thirty-five have had some direct contact with discussions about our faith or teaching about the quilt's content. The project has fostered tremendous dialogue about what faith means to us."

In April 2006, the Faith Quilts Project held an exhibition titled "Faith, the Arts, and Community" at the Boston Center for the Arts' Cyclorama, where the quilts were on display before going on a brief tour to five sites throughout Boston. Participants explored the theme of faith through music, film, poetry and dance. From there, Wainwright and the Faith Quilts Project team have created resource materials about the project, in hopes that people in other cities will begin a quilt or use the materials created in Boston as a starting point for dialogue about faith.

"We want to stir up an ongoing conversation around faith in all its ramifications, about the human spirit and what it seeks in life," Wainwright says. ♥

The Faith Quilts Project
P.O. Box 256
Scituate, MA 02066
Ph: 781.545.5707
www.faithquilts.org

The Pluralism Project
Committee on the Study of Religion
Harvard University
1531 Cambridge Street
Cambridge, MA 02139
Ph: 617.496.2481
www.pluralism.org

Public Conversations Project (PCP)
46 Kondazian Street
Watertown, MA 02472
Ph: 617.923.1216
www.publicconversations.org
Promotes constructive conversations and relationships among people who have differing values, world views and perspectives about divisive public issues.

LANTERN ON TROUT LAKE DURING THE ILLUMINARES LANTERN PROCESSION.

PHOTO BY T. SCHREDD.

OPPOSITE: PARADE OF THE LOST SOULS, FIRE PERFORMERS.

PHOTO BY N. STRIDER.

Coming Home

Public Dreams goes back to the village

KATE MADDEN YEE

Dusk. Under a shower of fireworks, the crowd starts to move around the lake, guided by four processional bands. Drummers dance with joyful abandon as they lead the way. Bamboo and tissue paper lanterns light the path, ranging from simple box shapes to the truly light fantastic: a twelve-foot whale, an eight-foot lion, a six-foot champagne flute; flamingos, butter-flies, dinosaurs, fairies, witches, and castles; a Stonehenge replica, the Mad Hatter's tea party, and even a line of laundry hanging between two trees. It's Illuminares, a festival of light celebrated every summer on the shores of Trout Lake in Vancouver, British Columbia, Canada.

"I love the creativity, love coming here to see what everyone has done," one woman says, her lantern and her enthusiasm lighting her face. "It's every kind of people, they come from everywhere, and they come to take a chance on magic."

The people behind Illuminares are the artists of Public Dreams Society, a visionary Vancouver-based group that works to create magical events, traditions, and rituals that promote community participation in the arts and healthy neighborhoods. For twenty years, Public Dreams has produced several hundred events in Western Canada alone, and many more across the entire country. In addition to the lantern festival, the organization puts on Parade of Lost Souls, a celebration of the dead and the living, and a circus called Circus of Dreams. They are also known for The Fire Box, an ongoing theatrical performance ritual that incorporates fire sculpture, lantern-installations, shrines, stilt dancing, torch choreography, and fire dancing, music and storytelling.

T-REX PUPPET MAKES FRIENDS AT THE VANCOUVER INTERNATIONAL CHILDREN'S FESTIVAL, HELD ANNUALLY IN MAY.

Public Dreams

Although Public Dreams events started small, they've grown since their inception. For example, in 1989, their first Illuminares drew about 300 people; today 30,000 gather at Trout Lake Park with as many as 8,000 handmade lanterns.

"Illuminares is for all ages, all walks of life, all cultural groups," says Dolly Hopkins, one of the founding members of Public Dreams and its artistic director. "In fact, since it's a visual experience with no dialogue, each person gets to write their own script, and decide what the ritual means to them."

Public Dreams began when performing artist Hopkins and colleagues Paula Jardine and Leslie Fiddler—also performing artists—came together over tea in Hopkins's kitchen and began to dream about launching community art events in Vancouver. Hopkins had been performing a one-woman show throughout the 1980s, and was looking for something new.

"I wanted more creative possibilities in my life, a bigger challenge," she says. "I recognized that people were losing touch with who they were, and that essence of who we are was being ground down by television, computers. We were driving ourselves away from the creative with our focus on the cognitive, and forgetting something important in the process."

The idea was to create celebrations that would spark connection among neighbors and allow Vancouverites to play together through performances, festivals and rituals, as well as offer other local artists employment and mentorship. By recreating a version of the village—an ancient human grouping where people share cultural ideas, music, story and costume—the women hoped to tap into a connection between people they believed was being degraded. Later that year, the Public Dreams Society was born.

"We wanted to go back to the village, go back in human history when people lived together in communities and were connected because they needed each other," Hopkins says. "All of us have a DNA imprint of being mythmakers, storytellers, musicians. It's part of who we are, but we can't recognize it in ourselves anymore. We've disassociated from it through time and history."

To raise awareness and participation, Public Dreams staff offers workshops at community centers, church halls and private homes in the months leading up to the event. Here, people learn how to make lanterns for Illuminares or costumes for the Parade of Lost Souls.

Key to Public Dreams' success is its group of volunteers, which include a core of about 70 regulars but swells to 500 as events approach. As the scope of the celebrations have grown, that basic grassroots structure of "you call five friends, I'll call five friends" doesn't work like it used to. In its place, Public Dreams has developed its own flexible but organized structure that allows events to run smoothly, with the help of professional volunteer managers. "Volunteers are screened, mentored and trained, and offered as much responsibility as they want," says Heidi Taylor, volunteer manager. "Our volunteers are enthusiastic because there's so much freedom to make things happen. There's room to bring a new idea and run with

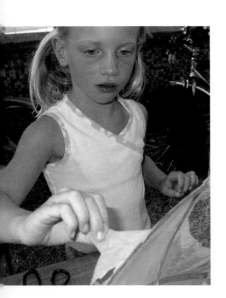

YOUNG GIRL GLUING AT
LANTERN MAKING WORKSHOP.
PHOTO BY S. KOBIALKA.

it. People come in knowing very little and within a short period take on leadership roles. They get a chance to do things they've never done before."

Carmen Perez Bielby of Vancouver has worked with Public Dreams on the Illuminares festival for seven years. A stay-at-home mom who volunteers with several organizations, she mentors groups that include teenagers volunteering with Public Dreams for a school project, and retirees interested in exploring a new skill. Her own lanterns have included a dancing girl, a flock of flamingos and an alligator that floats on the lake.

LANTERNS HANGING AFTER
WORKSHOP EVENT.
PHOTO BY S. KOBIALKA

"There's something that's always fresh for me, no matter what age group I'm working with," Bielby says. "People come in and, even though they feel they're not artists, they start growing within themselves as they create a lantern. I love seeing that gleam in their eyes when a drawing they've done on paper comes to life."

The events offer people a chance to play in ways that are not easy to find in our culture, says Katharine Carol, associate artistic director of Public Dreams and director of Illuminares.

"It's my belief that the more rigid we get, the more controlled, the more we need to allow ourselves space to let loose," she says. "Our events offer people an opportunity to do that safely, to connect with each other in a non-cerebral, more physical way."

What started as three women talking in a Vancouver

kitchen has grown into a way of working with communities all across Canada: Now more than forty-seven events are produced each year in communities that have been mentored by Public Dreams staff. Through its growth and success, Public Dreams still retains its creative core.

"Watch a child when she's doing something with pure innocence, presence and intent," Carol says. "It gives you a good feeling. Public Dreams events give people that same feeling. They get to play with innocence and presence, taking time away from the multitasking world. It's magic." ♥

Public Dreams
141-2050 Scotia Street
Vancouver, British Columbia
Canada V5T 4T1
Ph: 604.879.8611
www.publicdreams.org

OPPOSITE: "THE FISH" BY
SONA ALLAHVERDIEVA,
AGE 6. BAKU, AZERBAIJAN.
PALACE OF CHILDREN AND
YOUTH CREATIVE WORK.
TEACHER: TATYANA KESAR
© RIVER OF WORDS

ARTISTIC DIRECTOR
OF PUBLIC DREAMS,
DOLLY HOPKINS

ARTIST AS ACTIVIST

"CROWDED POND" BY MARIE ZHANG, AGE 11

WEST LAFAYETTE, INDIANA. FANG'S ART SCHOOL.

TEACHER: C.J. FANG. © RIVER OF WORDS

River of Words

The language of landscape

PAMELA MICHAEL

River of Words has come a long way since 1995 when then-U.S. Poet Laureate Robert Hass and I and a group of poets, educators, artists, river activists and booksellers began meeting weekly above a pizza parlor in Berkeley, California. Our goal was to blend poetry, art, nature study, watershed awareness, community service, history and critical thinking into a flexible, simple and elegant curriculum for schoolchildren. We called our project River of Words. We'd hoped to cause a few ripples in the education world; in fact, we unleashed a deluge.

Our motivation was a disturbing study that indicated that while children in the United States could identify over a thousand corporate logos, few could recognize and name more than a handful of the plants that grew in their own neighborhoods. As a nation we have—within our lifetimes—lost our understanding of the natural world, our sense of connection and belonging to a particular place. This fragmentation of landscapes and cultural threads is being repeated throughout the world.

The River of Words International Youth Poetry & Art Contest was created to help children regain an intimacy with the web of life and to develop a rich and sustaining "language of landscape." We hoped that by studying their particular watershed—the contest's annual theme—and the art and literature it has inspired, children could discover their place in a wider community, learn about their region's history and literature, local flora and fauna, indigenous traditions and much more.

Today, River of Words (ROW) is an educational nonprofit organization that conducts, in affiliation with the Library of Congress Center for the Book, the world's largest youth poetry and art contest. Each year we train hundreds of educators—classroom teachers, park rangers, youth leaders and others—on ways to incorporate nature exploration and the arts into their work with young people with the help of our "Watershed Explorer" curriculum.

ROW encourages students around the world to explore their own communities and imaginations—weaving in natural and cultural history—and then to synthesize what they've learned and observed into line and verse. Our hope is that focusing students' attention on their own home grounds will give them an informed understanding of place that will help them grow into engaged citizens. We've tried to add elements of wonder, discovery, interpretation, dexterity and surprise to learning, and to promote the idea that while not everyone can be an artist, everyone can be artistic.

Each year contest entries pour in to our Berkeley office from a wide cross-section of America's youth: from public, private and parochial schools representing nearly every state, from home-schooling families, after-school programs, 4-H, Girl Scouts, nature centers, youth clubs and libraries. We accept poems in English, Spanish and (on videotape) American Sign

Language. We receive entries from many other countries, too—Afghanistan, Australia, Bangladesh, China, England, Ghana, Kenya, Israel, Pakistan, Azerbaijan, just to name a few. The contest is free to enter; all entrants receive a "Watershed Explorer" certificate.

Our "Watershed Explorer" curriculum guide (K-12) encourages teachers to partner with other teachers in their school—a science teacher and an English teacher, for example—as well as others outside the school—bird-watchers, writers, park rangers, water department employees, photographers, farmers and such. Even though most communities have citizens who might jump at the chance to take kids on a field trip or give a classroom presentation, most school systems have no vehicle for engaging such people. One doesn't just knock on the schoolhouse door and say, "I know how to read animal tracks" or "I can identify all our native plants." River of Words, from the start, was as much about building community partnerships as it was about education, nature and the arts.

Many communities have developed innovative ways of implementing River of Words. One small town in New Mexico celebrated with a River of Words parade down Main Street, replete with streetlight banners made by local children of their artwork. Every shop in town that day had a basket next to the cash register where one could leave or take a poem. The community also sponsored a riverbank clean-up and poetry reading, which has become an annual event. In Michigan, a bookstore owner sponsored a River of Words evening for teachers at her store. She invited representatives of all the local groups and agencies that had watershed programs or materials to meet with teachers and discuss how to use their resources.

In California, an elementary teacher added a multigenerational aspect to River of Words by having her class visit a senior citizen home that stood alongside a creek. The

students conducted oral history interviews of the elders, many of whom were lifelong residents of the area. They explored the creek together, then returned to their classrooms to write poems and paint. When the seniors received copies of the children's work they were so inspired that they invited the class to return with their families and the teacher the following month. To the surprise of the students, the seniors threw them a party and read poems they had written in response to the children's work. Many were about the creek, and quite a few included their own childhood memories of the place. The teacher now takes her class to the senior home every year; and every year, in town after town, more and more local events are sparked by River of Words—events that build community awareness and support ongoing partnerships in support of education, conservation and the arts.

Clearly, the children who participate in River of Words each year have gained much. In addition to learning the ecology and value of their watersheds, their imaginations find much to celebrate, honor and nurture. Robert Hass, the contest's co-founder, and now co-chair of the board of directors, believes that neither poetry nor science alone can make the next generation better stewards of the earth. "We need both things—a living knowledge of the land and a live imagination of it and our place in it—if we are going to preserve it," he said. "Good science and a vital art and, in the long run, wisdom."

River of Words has become a partner of the Center for the Book at the Library of Congress. For almost a decade, the Center for the Book has played host to the annual awards ceremony for the grand prize winners and their families. The contest accepts entries from children all over the world and honors an international grand prize winner at the Library ceremony, as well as eight winners from the U.S. and a Teacher of the Year.

Winning entries are published annually in "River of Words: The Natural World as Viewed by Young People." The children's work is exhibited all over the world at museums, national parks, schools, libraries and other venues. We also conduct teacher-training workshops and maintain a network of thirty-plus state coordinators, often housed at state departments of natural resources, or libraries. Many states conduct their own River of Words' contests in conjunction with the larger contest.

To showcase a growing collection of extraordinary art and poetry, River of Words in 2003 opened "Young at Art," one of the first art galleries in the country devoted to children's art from around the world. We also recently opened a Creative Learning Lab adjacent to our Berkeley gallery and office. The Lab offers classes for children and families in art, writing, science and a variety of other disciplines.

River of Words benefits not only the children who participate in our programs and their communities—others are catching on to the power of these images and poems, too. The U.S. EPA has used them to enliven several publications, including its bi-annual Report to Congress. In California, the Department of Fish and Game includes ROW art and poetry in a permanent display at the Nimbus Fish Hatchery near Sacramento. The town of Walnut Creek has inscribed a ROW poem on a downtown sculpture.

Can there be any doubt that education is the key to sustainable living, tolerance and a peaceful world? We offer these thoughtful and heartfelt creations from the children of the world as our best hope for the future. ♥

"RIVER OF WORDS"
BY LIM YI FAN, AGE 11
PERAK, MALAYSIA.
TEACHER: ANCY NG
© RIVER OF WORDS

berwick

I am from the brown water in a lake caged

From the Corps' walls that greet the sun

I am from the cabin on the water

And the hand-built dock, littered with extensions of friends

I am from the tall cypress that move with the wind

From the hushed conversations the willows have with morning

I am from the fog off the water

And the winds from the south

I am from wax myrtles, hydrangeas and the scent of burnt sulfur.

I am from the mismatched eyes of our faithful Catahoula

And the crisp boat rides, trying to outrun December's chill

I am from the Basin, watching the sun fall below the wall of man

Billy Creed, age 16
Denham Springs, Louisiana

"I GOT THE BLUES" BY GERALD ALLEN, AGE 13.

BROADMOOR MIDDLE MAGNET SCHOOL

BATON ROUGE, LOUISIANA.

TEACHER: ALAN MORTON

© RIVER OF WORDS

Why I Teach Poetry

ALICIA HOKANSON

Each year we take a trip with our sixth graders to a piece of old growth forest preserved in West Seattle. When we enter the forest of Schmitz Park, the first thing we do is place each student in his or her own special spot along the trail: above the creek on a rock, underneath a huge cedar or on top of an uprooted hemlock that has become a nurse log. Each student has time for silent observation, opening eyes and ears and fingertips to their sensory world and recording what they experience. Each year they surprise me anew. They hear deeper, see farther, play longer with the language to say what they've seen. They are newer to the world and its wonder is not dimmed for them. Claire hears streams pound, sink, blend. Their swishilling sound wafts through every leaf. Eliot sees a gibbering creek riding down the forest, sparkling in the sun's hot rays. Leah feels the eerie presence of nothingness radiating from every forest object. Kate writes, "I rest my mind in the calm of nature."

After these solos in the forest, we gather everyone for a scavenger hunt to find and name the native plants they've studied in science. Who can find those pesky nettles, or the firm silky leaves of salal, or point out Oregon grape, big leaf maple, western red cedar and tell us how they know them? When they do recognize the nettles by the trail, the braver ones will fold a leaf inward, curling it, then pluck it and pop it in their mouths. Mr. Jamieson has shown them how to approach a nettle and not get stung! A few kids, recognizing the soft leaves of thimbleberry, will also find red caps still ripe for eating. This touching, tasting and naming of things in the forest is a crucial start for our poets.

A first lesson: not "tree" but the name—fir, alder, maple, pine—hearing the sounds and the music in the specific, and tasting the word on the tongue. Not "flower," but nootka rose, anemone, columbine. In their writer's notebooks they've started recording their observations, fuel for poems later.

Closer to school, we explore our neighborhood Thornton Creek watershed. In October we head out with knee-high boots and rain gear, with clipboards and plastic sheets. Rain or shine we'll observe, listen, smell, touch and write. We stop frequently along the way: from the swampy section of the creek as it daylights after running under Northgate shopping mall to the free full-flowing creek at Matthews Beach where it flows into Lake Washington. We see mallards, kingfishers, heron, a few returning salmon and find lots of muck to stomp in. Our almost-teenagers are just eleven-year-old kids today, wading out into the lake until, inevitably, the water comes over their boot tops and they shriek.

Before we leave, there's time to sit at the edge of the creek and write together. A recent group poem:

> I flee from a machinery world
> Leaving worries behind. At the creek
> the flowing waters form a bridge between worlds.
> Sun glows through the trees and its reflection
> is like a pathway to heaven.
>
> Under grey sky, under gold leaves
> dark birches are wavering
> on the surface of the creek.
> A trickle of water shimmers
> as it dances over the rocks
> creating a waterfall,
> changing the pace of the world.

"TREAT BY THE RIVER"

BY CATHERINE RIVARD, AGE 14

ARLINGTON, MINNESOTA

© RIVER OF WORDS

Returning to school we're suddenly back in the clatter of returning clipboards, stacking piles of soggy papers, hosing off boots and racing to lunch! By January we are reading T'ang dynasty poems and Japanese haiku. The students immediately take to these forms with their close dependence on images of the natural world. They understand the ancient impulse and find their voices taking up again the old song of praise.

Joseph writes: green moss on a rock / water-christened / deep in the rain-draped ravine. Madeline sees: sheets of rain / the cherry blossoms turn skyward / to drink. And Leo knows how to win an English teacher's heart. His first haiku is an ars poetica: Capture the moment / Observe nature as best you can / Preserve the image.

Perhaps this gives you a sense of why I love sharing poetry with middle-schoolers and encourage them to write it. They are not jaded, they notice more than I think they will, they continually surprise me, they are still in the world with all their senses, and, like sponges, they soak up what each poem they read has to teach.

Why do I teach poetry? Because I want poets running my neighborhood council, my city, my country. I want poets tuned to the changes of light and season, who know the names of all the birds and will notice if fewer of them return in spring. I teach poetry because I want a richer world for all of us—where the truths of the eye and the heart are valued more than those of the pocketbook. Where students who experience the balance of a mind at rest in nature will turn away from war as a solution to anything. I want my world governed by writers/thinkers/feelers like Madeline who can feel as sharply as those ancient masters, LiPo and DuFu, the pangs of loss when in autumn the geese depart, and who know the experience of loss resonates in every human soul. I teach poetry because I know it teaches us to enlarge our compassion for all peoples and creatures, for all of nature in its renewing beauty. ♥

river of words and watershed resources

River of Words
(and **Young at Art Gallery**)
2547 8th Street, 13B
Berkeley, CA 94710
www.riverofwords.org
Ph: 510.348.POEM (7636)

River of Words: Images and Poetry in Praise of Water
Pamela Michael, Editor
Introductory Essays by Robert Hass and Thacher Hurd
Heyday Books, Berkeley, CA
www.heydaybooks.com

This Odyssey: Poetic Quests of a Teenage Girl
by Jane Jiang, high school senior and 2002 River of Words Grand Prize winner. Jane is donating proceeds of the book to Hurricane Katrina relief.

Center for Watershed Protection
www.cwp.org

EPA Web Sites
Wetlands, Oceans, & Watershed
www.epa.gov/owow

Surf Your Watershed
www.epa.gov/surf

Adopt Your Watershed
www.epa.gov/adopt

River Network
520 SW 6th Avenue, Portland, OR 97204
Ph: 503.241.3506
www.rivernetwork.org

"ENJOYING NATURE" BY KWOK YEN YI,
AGE 9, HONG KONG, CHINA. TEACHERS:
CHUI FAN LEE AND HOO CHEONG LAU
© RIVER OF WORDS

Cross-pollinating the Grassroots

The busy, busy Beehive Collective

A BEE FRIEND

THE REMOTE NEW ENGLAND TOWN OF MACHIAS, Maine, may not be the first place you'd expect to find a cluster of well-traveled, political-activist, graphic artists. The Beehive Design Collective, an all-volunteer group of wildly motivated young people, have created quite a buzz internationally and within their rural community in "Downeast" Maine.

The collective, known as "the Bees," has, in five short years achieved notoriety in political, educational and artistic circles for their impossibly detailed, monochrome posters about corporate globalization. These large format fabric murals take visual excursions through underbelly issues of global trade and the dominance of transnational corporations. With discourse in the form of colossal banners, the Bees regularly "swarm" throughout the Americas presenting interactive visual lectures. And, to the astonishment of the local Machias community, this group of youth from distant urban neighborhoods has poured long sweaty hours and slow-won resources into restoring their historic farmers Grange Hall. Miraculously, the entirety of the Bees' prodigious work has been funded only through speaker's fees, the sale of posters and individual donations.

The repertoire of the Beehive Design Collective addresses a diversity of themes ranging from sustainable agriculture, resource extraction, privatization and food sovereignty to global economic policy and U.S. militarization. To create their giant posters, collective members draw (literally) upon the accounts of those most affected by the subject of their campaigns, traveling often to Latin America to gather stories through an ethnographic style of research. During and after marathon interview sessions, the Bees create "mind-maps" —graphic frames of information over which they weave a

ONE OF THE COLLECTIVE'S FIRST WORKS: MONARCH BUTTERFLIES DON GAS-MASKS TO WARD OFF THE EFFECTS OF GENETICALLY MODIFIED CORN POLLEN, CONSIDERED A THREAT TO THIS VALUABLE POLLINA-TOR IN NORTH AMERICA.

tapestry of related stories. It's not unusual for brainstorming sessions to stretch from hours to days on end.

The Bees are compulsively attentive to the minutia. Visits to botanical societies to examine species of plants featured in their drawings are common, and all ideas and facts are critiqued methodically through a collaborative review process with the people depicted. This helps the Bees eliminate subtle racist assumptions, cultural appropriation and a myopic North American perspective. As a part of their strategy the Bees don't draw humans, rather the characters that inhabit their meticulous illustrations are all animals, insects and plants indigenous

ABOVE: A BEE METICULOUSLY INKS THE NINE-FOOT-TALL ORIGINAL OF THE *PLAN COLOMBIA* GRAPHIC.

RIGHT: A TWO-TIERED PAPER WASP NEST REPRESENTS COLONIZATION IN THE *PLAN COLOMBIA* GRAPHIC. GHOST WASPS SWARM FROM A EUROPEAN-SHAPED NEST TO THE SHORES OF NORTH AMERICA, BRINGING WITH THEM WEAPONS, DISEASE AND EUROPEAN CONCEPTS OF TIME.

ABOVE: USING A LARGE FAB-
RIC FLIPBOOK AND 30-FOOT
BANNER, TWO BEES PRESENT
THE *PLAN COLOMBIA* PICTURE
LECTURE TO A CROWD DUR-
ING A WEEK-LONG RESIDENCY
AT PACIFIC NORTHWEST COL-
LEGE OF ART IN PORTLAND,
OREGON.

LEFT: LADYBUGS PLANNING
AND AT WORK ON GRANGE
MEETING HALL RENOVATION
(*SEE PAGE 127*).

UPPER RIGHT: ANTS IN AGRI-
CULTURAL HARVEST SCENE.

to the regions portrayed. The tools and garb used by characters are critical clues to their identity. This allows the Bees to avoid creating stereotyped, "Disneyfied" caricatures of race, culture or body type.

The Beehive collaborative graphics are empowering tools for teaching and organizing. More than amazing art, their posters communicate narratives of depth. Their early work focused first on biotechnology and genetic engineering. Then the notion of engineering was broadened to depict a corporate tendency of homogenizing society itself. In 2001, the Bees embarked on the creation of a trilogy to galvanize awareness on issues of globalization. The first part of this nearly completed project was a poster about the proposed Free Trade Areas of the Americas (FTAA), a hemispheric mega-commerce initiative. From a wide-angle perspective on trade dynamics and its many repercussions, the Bees' trilogy zooms in on a cross-section of *Plan Colombia*, the official moniker of the U.S.-financed "War on Drugs." The poster is reminiscent of a scroll, unfurling from the top down. It portrays, as a mosquito swarm, tiers of advanced military equipment descending above the horrific wake of a routine chemical fumigation of the Amazon rainforest, purportedly to annihilate the coca leaf. Animals, insects, machinery and molecular structures cascade in a tumult while the protagonists, rendered as leaf-cutter ants, scramble over the surface of the drawing to dismantle puzzle-pieces of the nightmare imagery.

The finale of the trilogy, tentatively titled *Mesoamerica Resiste* stands as the epitome of the Bees' work. The campaign focuses on *Plan Puebla Panamá*, a proposed infrastructure development program of epic proportions that would drastically alter the face of Central America. Over 200 species of animals, plants and insects inhabit the fold-out triptych. To inform this graphic, a swarm of ten Bees journeyed from Puebla, Mexico, to Panama over the course of five months in the spring of 2004, gathering stories of resistance from over 180 groups and individuals. Members of the Beehive Collective are busy completing the illustration, now two years in process. When complete, graphics in the trilogy will be condensed into a teacher's coloring book curriculum on corporate globalization.

"With our graphics," explain the Bees, "there's a high degree of interactivity. When someone presents the poster, they become the storyteller of the work." The posters are understandable across lines of age, language and culture, with a minimum of text. When the Bees travel, they present their

BEES PRESENTING *PLAN COLOMBIA* PICTURE LECTURE TO A HIGHLY INTERACTIVE CROWD OF STUDENTS AT A TEACHER'S TRAINING SCHOOL IN LA ESPERANZA, HONDURAS, 2004.

illustrated campaigns in huge banner-prints in conjunction with either six-foot-tall fabric picture books or projected slides that show enlarged details from the posters. Participants are invited to ask questions and share their own thoughts or knowledge on the subject.

The Collective has an opposite stance from the hyper-individualism that characterizes a territorial "art world;" they are anti-copyright, and encourage the free reproduction of their work for non-profit use. After their presentations, they encourage participants to take the story themselves and conduct their own picture lectures when showing the posters to others. "The information is very mobile," one Bee adds. "Someone may not remember the whole story, but seeing a piece of the drawing later helps orient them to what's going on."

While the Collective is often hard at work on the road—either gathering information for their graphic campaigns, or running speaking tours—the Bees hardly rest when back at home in Washington County, Maine. The economic blight that this easternmost part of the country has suffered as a result of reliance on heavy extraction of natural resources (timber and fishing) is a reminder to the Bees of the dangers of insensitive industrialization—exactly what they are working to prevent in Latin America.

PEOPLE FROM NEAR AND FAR CIRCLE UP
DURING ONE OF THE MANY DISCUSSIONS
AND WORKSHOPS THAT OCCURRED DURING
THE MACHIAS GRANGE'S 100TH BIRTHDAY
AND REBIRTH CELEBRATION.

THE PENNELS—LONG TIME MEMBERS
OF THE MAINE STATE GRANGE.

In May of 2001 the Collective purchased Machias Valley Grange Hall, a handsome structure built above the town's waterfalls some 100 years ago that had long sat empty in disrepair. Although their first motive was to find an appropriate home and workspace for their own operation, the Bees initially did not know they would rescue more than the meeting hall from demolition, for in the process of restoring this neglected building, they helped rebuild community culture and gave the town back a center that all generations now enjoy.

Together with local farmers and volunteers from across the country (respondents to the Bees' invitations during their speaking tours), the Bees were able to complete the renewal of the Grange Hall. In epic bursts of summertime energy over five years, volunteer Bee teams pressure-washed, installed a new roof and chimney, painted interior and exterior, and restored elegant features like the Hall's tin ceiling and hardwood floor. The renovated façade became a local wonder.

"Everyone was really surprised to see us hanging off the side of the building on scaffolding all day," remarked a Bee. "We were there before most folks' morning commute. And we saw them driving home—we were there late into the night."

August 20th, 2005 marked the end of the summer-long marathons. The doors of the Machias Valley Grange Hall swung open to the community during the Washington County Wild Blueberry Festival, with speakers and musicians overflowing in the weekend's festivities. After an open-invite community potluck, the floor was yielded to the Machias Valley Grangers.

VOLUNTEERS INSTALL A NEW METAL ROOF TO THE GRANGE HALL. STATE TRANSPORTATION PLANNING HAS REMOVED MUCH OF THE LAND ON THE BUILDING'S NE CORNER, LEAVING NO BUFFER BETWEEN TRAFFIC AND THE EDIFICE.

A packed Hall with over 200 people from near and far, includ-ing the state Grangemaster, witnessed the heartfelt homecom-ing of Grange #360. Vivian Thaxter, ninety-four years of age, spoke about what a magical place the Hall was for her—here she had joined the Grange seventy-five years ago, and here, too, she had met her husband.

"The Grange means a lot to our community," said one attendee. "It's been a part of so many people's lives. It's great to see it come back to life!" Paperwork is in process to commit the building to the National Register of Historic Places.

And where did the Bees go, now that their de facto home was opened to the town? Three years of searching led to the purchase of yet another historic building, just weeks before the Grange celebration. The Clark Perry House, five minutes across the Machias waterfalls, is the new live/work space of the Collective, fitting their needs perfectly. A registered historic place and a marvel of architecture, the home once belonged to the town's timber baron and tax collector, an ironic contrast to the Grange's legacy. Through overwhelming and unanticipated support from the sellers and regional financial institutions, the Bees were able to secure a mortgage on another of Machias' most distinguished buildings.

The Beehive also is known for original stone mosaic murals, in fact the Beehive Collective actually began as an all-women's stone mosaic cooperative: original members in need of help issued a call for assistance to complete an expansive stonework commission, the response surpassed their expecta-tions, and membership swelled. Since then, over twenty-five apprentices have learned how to create custom-cut, handmade mosaic murals from marble and granite. As with their illustrat-ed graphic campaigns, the Bees populate these enduring images with animals and insects, many of which are endangered. The Bees continue to create mosaics, and offer an apprenticeship program to interested parties to sustain the craft. Their collection of self-made mosaics leaves Machias once per year to go on display at the Maine Organic Farmers and Gardeners Association's hugely popular country fair. There, it is displayed next to an interactive mosaic, which visitors to the Bees' booth are encouraged to participate in making.

The future holds much for the Beehive Design Collective. The Bees say they want to foster anti-copyright visual arts that resonate with social and environmental consciousness. Other illustrated campaigns are on the horizon after the release of "*Mesoamerica Resiste*," and they anticipate using their new home to host a political artists' residency and retreat program. Indeed, the Bees maintain that there isn't ever a finish line for the work they do. ♥

Beehive Design Collective
www.beehivecollective.org
pollinators@beehivecollective.org

A MOSAIC APPRENTICE FORMS THE
COMPONENTS OF A STONE MURAL
BY SHAPING FRAGMENTS OF MARBLE
BY HAND WITH ERGONOMIC NIPPERS.
MOSAICS PROJECTS BROUGHT THE
ORIGINAL GROUP OF SIX BEES, ALL
YOUNG WOMEN, TOGETHER.

community-based arts resources

Alternate Roots
1083 Austin Avenue, NE
Atlanta, GA 30307
Ph: 404.577.1079
www.alternateroots.org
Supports arts rooted in a particular community of place, tradition or spirit. Programs address concerns of social and economic justice and protection of the natural world. Quarterly publication "Up From the Roots" is distributed nationally.

American Association for Theatre and Education
7475 Wisconsin Avenue, Suite 300A
Bethesda, MD 20814
Ph: 301.951.7977
www.aate.com
Advocates for theater and education, promoting highest standards and providing networking opportunities for exchange and diversification of practices, audiences and perspectives.

Americans for the Arts
1000 Vermont Avenue NW, 6th Floor
Washington, DC 20005
Ph: 202.371.2830
One East 53rd Street, 2nd Floor
New York, NY 10022
Ph: 212.223.2787
www.artsusa.org
Advancing the arts in America. Focuses on three primary goals: increasing public and private sector support for the arts; ensuring that every American child has access to a high-quality arts education; and strengthening communities through the arts.

Animating Democracy
www.artsusa.org/animatingdemocracy
Developed by Americans for the Arts and the Ford Foundation to profile and build capacity of artists and organizations whose work engages the public in dialogue.

Appalshop
91 Madison Avenue
Whitesburg, KY 41858
Ph: 606.633.0108
www.appalshop.org
Multi-disciplinary arts and education center in Appalachia producing original artwork based on the proposition that the world is immeasurably enriched when local cultures tell their own stories and listen to the stories of others.

Art in the Public Interest (API)
www.apionline.org
www.communityarts.net
P.O. Box 68
Saxapahaw, NC 27340
Ph: 336.376.8404
Supports the belief that the arts are an integral part of a healthy culture, and that community-based arts provide significant value to both communities and artists. Manages the Community Arts Network.

Arts & Culture Indicators in Community Building Project
www.urban.org/nnip/acip.htm
Project of National Neighborhood Indicators Partnership (NNIP). It is an exploratory effort to develop arts and culture neighborhood indicators for use in local planning, policymaking and community building.

Artspace Projects
250 Third Avenue North, Suite 500
Minneapolis, MN 55401
www.artspaceusa.org
Nonprofit real-estate developer for the arts, with more than a dozen completed projects across the United States. Asset management, property management, resource development, consulting.

Arts and Healing Network
www.artheals.org
Extensive on-line resource for exploring the healing potential of art and to celebrate the connection between arts and healing.

Association of Performing Arts Presenters
1112 16th Street NW, Suite 400
Washington, DC 20036
Ph: 202.833.2787
www.artspresenters.org
Membership organization bringing performers and audiences together in every way imaginable. Provides visionary thinking, professional development, resource sharing and advocacy.

Center for Art and Public Life
California College of the Arts
5212 Broadway, Oakland, CA 94618
Ph: 510.594.3763
http://center.cca.edu
Focuses on important issues in community development, service learning in arts education, new models of practice in community-based arts, and cultural diversity and youth development through the arts.

Centre for Creative Communities
Regent House Business Centre
24/25 Nutford Place, Marble Arch
London W1H 5YN, UK
Ph: 020.7569.3005
www.creativecommunities.org.uk

Promotes civic engagement through dialogue among community, public and corporate sectors. Facilitates collaborative community development projects utilizing the arts, culture and heritage. Offers publications.

Center for Digital Storytelling
www.storycenter.org
1803 Martin Luther King Jr. Way
Berkeley CA 94709
Ph: 510.548.2065
Rooted in the art of personal storytelling, the Center assists in using the tools of digital media to craft, record, share and value the stories of individuals and communities, in ways that improve all lives.

Center for the Study of Art and Community
4566 Tangleberry Lane N.E.
Bainbridge Island, WA 98110
Ph: 206.855.0977
www.artandcommunity.com
An association of creative leaders from business, government and the arts who have succeeded in building bridges between the arts and a wide range of community, public and private sector interests.

Community Arts Network (CAN)
www.communityarts.net
An extensive online resource of projects, programs and journalism that actively promotes the arts as part of education, political life, health recovery, prisoner rehabilitation, environmental protection, community regeneration, electronic communication and more.

Culture Shapes Community
1429 21st Street, NW
Washington, DC 20036
Ph: 202.276.6503
www.cultureshapescommunity.org
Recognizes neighborhood cultural organizations as unique stakeholders in poor neighborhoods experiencing economic and demograph-
ic shifts. Programs promote social integration
among mixed-income and mixed-race residents, empowering all to have a strong voice
for equitable neighborhood change.

Folk Alliance
510 South Main Street, 1st floor
Memphis, TN 38103
Ph: 901.522.1170
www.folkalliance.net
Fosters traditional, contemporary and
multicultural folk music and dance in North
America. Strengthens organizational and
individual initiatives through education, networking, advocacy, and professional and field
development.

Front Porch Institute
964 17th Street, Astoria, OR 97103
www.patrickoverton.com
Explores the role of arts and culture in com-
munity-making process in rural and small
communities. Assists organizations and
individuals in understanding their own sense
of community and culture. Created by Patrick
Overton in 1996.

Green Arts Web
www.greenarts.org
Online resource provides information on practices and theories of environmental art, links
to community organizations and programs.

Intermedia Arts
2822 Lyndale Avenue South
Minneapolis, MN 55408
Ph: 612.871.4444
www.intermediaarts.org
Multi-disciplinary arts center, helping to
develop new art forms, which are artistically,
socially and politically challenging, believing
that the arts inspire and build a sense of community.

**Kennedy Center Alliance for Arts
Education Network**
John F. Kennedy Center for the Performing Arts
2700 F Street, NW
Washington, DC 20566
www.kennedy-center.org/education/kcaaen
A coalition to support policies, practices,
programs and partnerships that ensure the
arts are an essential part of American K-12
education.

**National Alliance for Media Arts
and Culture**
145 Ninth Street, Suite 205
San Francisco, CA 94103
Ph: 415.431.1391
www.namac.org
Membership association of over 350 independent media organizations and individuals.
Promotes media arts by providing education,
advocacy and opportunities for those in the
field to interact with their peers.

National Assembly of State Arts Agencies
1029 Vermont Avenue, NW, 2nd Floor
Washington, DC 20005
Ph: 202.347.6352
www.nasaa-arts.org
Gateway to the nation's 56 state and jurisdictional arts agencies, which it serves through strategic assistance with leadership, planning, decision-making and resources. Advances the meaningful role of the arts in private and public life.

National Center for Creative Aging (NCCA)
138 S. Oxford Street
Brooklyn, NY 11217
Ph: 718.398.3870
www.creativeaging.org
Fosters an appreciation of the vital relationship between creative expression and quality of life for older people of all cultures and ethnic backgrounds, regardless of economic status, age, or level of physical, emotional or cognitive functioning.

National Endowment for the Arts (NEA)
1100 Pennsylvania Avenue NW
Washington, DC 20506
Ph: 202.682.5400
www.nea.gov
Established by Congress in 1965 as an independent agency of the federal government, the NEA is the largest national funder of the arts. Supports excellence in the arts, and provides leadership in arts education and bringing the arts to all Americans.

National Guild of Community Schools for the Arts
520 8th Avenue, 3rd Floor, Suite 302
New York, NY 10018
Ph: 212.268.3337
www.nationalguild.org
Serves non-profit arts education organizations in urban, suburban and rural communities. Supports the creation of community art schools, providing research, professional development, advocacy and high-profile leadership.

National Performance Network (NPN)
New Orleans, LA
Ph: 504.595.8008
www.npnweb.org
Partnership of 55 arts organizations, across the U.S. connecting artists with communities to help make local neighborhood-based artwork, and to cross geographic and cultural divides to increase the traffic of fresh, challenging work.

National Storytelling Network (NSN)
132 Boone Street, Suite 5
Jonesborough, TN 37659
Ph: 800.525.4514 or 423.913.8201
www.storynet.org
Advances storytelling as a performing art, teaching aid and cultural transformation process. Offers direct services, publications and educational opportunities to individuals, local storytelling guilds and associations.

Network of Ensemble Theaters (NET)
c/o Irondale Ensemble Project
P.O. Box 150604
Brooklyn, NY 11215-0604
Ph: 718.488.9233
www.ensembletheaters.net
Consortium of North America's permanent ensemble companies committed to preserving the legacy of the ensemble theater movement.

Partners for Livable Communities
1429 21st Street, NW
Washington, DC 20036
Ph: 202.887.5990
www.livable.com
Provides several projects and publications based on the theory that creativity is essential to livable communities. Their "Culture Builds Communities" programs demonstrate how cultural resources can contribute to youth development, economic and social development, and community design.

Pedagogy & Theatre of the Oppressed (PTO)
P.O. Box 31623
Omaha, NE 68131-0623
www.ptoweb.org
Developed from ideology of Paulo Freire and Augusto Boal, to challenge oppressive systems by promoting critical thinking and social justice. Annual meeting focuses on the work of liberatory educators, activists, artists and community organizers.

Public Art Review
2324 University Avenue West, Suite 102
St. Paul, MN 55114
Ph: 651.641.1128
www.publicartreview.org
Project of FORECAST Public Artworks, is the only national journal focused on exploring the many dimensions of public art. Each issue provides coverage of growing trends, reflection on critical issues and the latest public art projects.

Raw Vision
163 Amsterdam Avenue, Suite 203
New York City, NY 10028-5001
Ph: 212.714.8381
www.rawvision.com
Quarterly international journal of the art of "unknown geniuses" who are creators of Outsider Art, Art Brut and Contemporary Folk Art.

Social and Public Art Resource Center (SPARC)
685 Venice Boulevard, Venice, CA 90291
Ph: 310.822.9560
www.sparcmurals.org/sparc
SPARC produces, preserves and conducts educational programs about community-based public art works. Espouses public art as an organizing tool for addressing contemporary issues, fostering cross-cultural understanding and promoting civic dialogue.

Social Impact of the Arts Project (SIAP)
University of Pennsylvania
School of Social Work
3701 Locust Walk, Philadelphia PA 19104-6214
www.ssw.upenn.edu/SIAP
Research Center that has undertaken a variety of policy research projects on the role cultural institutions play in the metropolitan Philadelphia region and neighborhoods.

Society for Creative Aging
2590 Walnut Street, Suite 11
Boulder, CO 80302
Ph: 303.440.8191
www.s4ca.org
Fosters understanding of the relationship between creative expression and healthy aging. Activities in the disciplines of visual arts, dance, music, film and theater. Annual festival.

Southern Arts Federation
1800 Peachtree Street NW, Suite 808
Atlanta, GA 30309
Ph: 404.874.7244
www.southarts.org
Assists in the professional development of artists, arts organizations and arts professionals. working in partnership with state arts agencies of Alabama, Florida, Georgia, Kentucky, Louisiana, Mississippi, North Carolina, South Carolina and Tennessee.

Theatre Communications Group
520 Eighth Avenue, 24th Floor
New York, NY 10018
Ph: 212.609.5900
www.tcg.org
TCG supports not-for-profit professional
American theater, with the goals of increasing
organizational efficiency of member theaters,
celebrating talent and achievements, and
promoting a larger public understanding of
the theater field.

U.S. Regional Arts Organizations
www.usregionalarts.org
Comprised of six regional non-profit entities
to support arts programs on a regional basis
and provide assistance to the state arts agencies. Funded by National Endowment for the
Arts, it supports arts organizations, artists and
communities through a wide range of regional,
multi-regional, national and international
funding programs. Website contains links to six
regional groups listed below and to state and
national arts agencies.
   Arts Midwest
   www.artsmidwest.org
   Mid-America Arts Alliance
   www.maaa.org
   Mid-Atlantic Arts Foundation
   www.midatlanticarts.org
   New England Foundation for the Arts
   www.nefa.org
   Western States Arts Federation
   www.westaf.org
   Southern Arts Federation
   www.southarts.org

VSA arts
818 Connecticut Avenue NW, Suite 600
Washington, DC 20006
Ph: 202.628.2800 or 800.933.8721
www.vsarts.org
Formerly Very Special Arts, national organization promoting inclusion in the arts for people
with disabilities

Youth Speaks
2169 Folsom Street S-100
San Francisco, CA 94110
Ph: 415.255.9035
www.youthspeaks.org
National youth poetry, spoken word, and
creative writing program. Projects include Teen
Poetry Slam, Brave New Voices, Bringing the
Noise Reading Series, Living Word Project and
writers-in-residence.

Zing Foundation
21 Linwood Street
Arlington, MA 02474
www.zings.org
Small organization (not a grantor) promoting
"out-of-the-box philanthropy" and strengthening the field of social healing arts.

Contributors

Heather Beal is a columnist, scriptwriter, poet and freelance journalist specializing in art, architecture, sustainability, business and cultural trends. She also lectures and serves on various boards and teams to promote the role of imagination in catalyzing positive social change. She was president of the board of directors of No Name Exhibitions during the period that the Soap Factory was renovated.

Tom Borrup is a consultant, writer and educator based in Minneapolis. He was executive director of Intermedia Arts from 1980 to 2002 and a trustee of the Jerome Foundation from 1994 to 2003. His book, *Creative Community Builders Handbook* will be published by Fieldstone Alliance.

Kiko Denzer lives with his family in Oregon's central coast range. He has introduced thousands of people, especially children, to the arts of earthen building. Kiko is the author of *Dig Your Hands in the Dirt: A Manual for Making Art Out of Earth* and *Build Your Own Earth Oven*, now in its seventh printing, For information on these and other books he publishes, visit Hand Print Press <www.handprintpress.com>.

Alicia Hokanson, a writing and poetry teacher at the Lakeside Middle School in Seattle, Washington, was named the River of Words Teacher of the Year in 2003. Her essay was excerpted from her acceptance speech at the Library of Congress.

Annie Rachele Lanzillotto was born in the Bronx of Barese heritage. Lanzillotto writes, performs, directs, curates, and, among other things, teaches the art of the Interaction Practitioner, which she developed from her Arthur Avenue Market project. She is a fellow of the Rockefeller Foundation's Next Generation Leadership Program, and her motto is: *forse sogniamo quasi abbastanza*....perhaps we dream nearly enough.

Author **Kate Madden Yee** is a founding member of Temescal Commons Cohousing in Oakland, California, established in 2000. Her favorite writing topics are women's health, spirituality and community-building.

Clare Cooper Marcus is Professor Emerita in the Departments of Architecture and Landscape Architecture at the University of California, Berkeley, where she initiated courses on social and psychological factors in the design of housing and public open space and now teaches a course on restorative landscapes. She is principal of the consulting firm Healing Landscapes in Berkeley and author and coauthor of several books, including *Healing Gardens* (Wiley and Sons, 1999).

Pamela Michael is executive director and co-founder of River of Words. She has been writing about education, community, the arts and travel for over twenty-five years, working with the United Nations, Save the Children and the Discovery Channel. Her writing and radio productions have won many awards.

Suzanne Young is an independent writer and editor based in San Francisco. Her work, which spans business journalism, profiles and personal essays, has appeared in the *San Francisco Chronicle Magazine* and *Forward Magazine*, among others. She is the author of *Beyond Engineering: How to Work on a Team.*

Index

new village press

The book you are holding was brought to you by New Village Press, the first publisher to serve the emerging field of community building. Communities are the cauldron of cultural development, and the healthiest communities grow from the grassroots. New Village publications focus on creative, citizen-initiated efforts—"the good news" of social change.

If you enjoyed *Works of Heart* you may be interested in other books we offer about community arts:

Beginner's Guide to Community-Based Arts
   by Mat Schwarzman, Keith Knight, Ellen Forney and others.
Performing Communities: Grassroots Ensemble Theaters Deeply Rooted in Eight U.S. Communities
   by Robert Leonard and Ann Kilkelly, edited by Linda Frye Burnham

Upcoming titles include:

New Creative Communities: The Art of Cultural Development
   by Arlene Goldbard
Art and Upheaval: Artists at Work on the World's Frontlines
   by William Cleveland
Building Commons and Community
   by the late Karl Linn

The Press is a project of Architects/Designers/Planners for Social Responsibility (www.adpsr.org), an educational nonprofit organization working for peace, environmental protection, social justice and the development of healthy communities.

See what else we publish: www.newvillagepress.net